INTRODUCTION

Reading hasn't always l
of traveling to and from
CD. Two of those bool
I view my parish; the ot~~~~~~ .... my life. Both
books were written by Ian Morgan Cron, the first entitled
Chasing Francis and the second, an autobiography entitled
Jesus, My Father, the CIA and me. I was so amazed at the
similarities between Cron and me that it made me think
seriously about my story, all those things in my life that
have formed the person I am today—my growing up years,
three marriages (yes, I said *three!*), raising children, the
ordination process—so many watershed events that have
brought me to this day in my life. And looking back, I'm
amazed at all the "God-incidences" that helped me choose
the various paths I've walked.

So, how do I begin? I've chosen to use the various places
I've lived as anchors throughout my story...you know,
those different places where I hung my hat for a time. Did
you know that according to statistics, the average number
of moves a person makes in a lifetime is seven? Today I'm
living in address number ten and each address represents a
time of major change, each one very different. Life is like
an old-fashioned clothes line, anchored on one side by
birth, the opposite side by eternity. And remember the long
poles we used to hoist up the clothesline so the clothes
wouldn't hit the ground once they were all hung on the
line? Well, my ten addresses represent ten poles under this
clothesline, each one hoping for a new beginning, a new
adventure, or possibly just another chance to get it right.

Then there are the *events*, the *experiences* that hang on that
clothesline, those things that made me who I am today.
And as I look at those experiences, I find myself saying, "If
only," or "Had I thought about it differently..." That's
called hindsight; surely, we've all been there. How
different so much of our lives would be if we had had the
benefit of hindsight. Today, however, even with hindsight,
I see so clearly how God was in control, taking even my
less thought-out decisions and poor choices and showing
me a better way, opening up a less traveled path where
there was none before.

My story is told with facts as I remember them, and I've added my thoughts in hindsight. Truth be told, God was at the helm from the beginning, whether I knew it or not, and even with my missteps, His plan was accomplished. I pray this reading will be encouraging to you.

"Before I formed you in the womb I knew you, and before you were born I consecrated you... For surely I know the plans I have for you, says the Lord, plans for your welfare and not for harm, but to give you a future of hope."
Jeremiah 1:5a, 29:11

CHAPTER 1

172 West Hooper Street
Tiverton, Rhode Island

> A typical new England home in the 1940s, white with red trim, two white pillars at the front door, a white picket fence; slanted ceilings on the second floor; the living room picture window facing a portion of Narragansett Bay, located on top of a hill.

One, one, forty-eight. I can't tell you how many times I have said that over the years. It was the answer to multiple questions: one, one, forty-eight. Every visit to a doctor, a tax office, the registry of motor vehicles, just to name a few. January 1, 1948. It's my birthday, and it's where my story begins. I'm not sure I know some of these things because I remember, someone told me or because it was captured on 8mm movie film. But, however I know it, there are lots of memories...

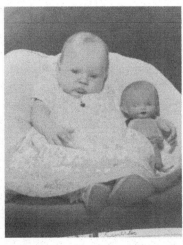

Elizabeth Ann Lane – 4 months

I was the youngest of four children. When I was born my two sisters were 12 and 20 and my brother was 19. Since my mother was in her late 30s and since my siblings were so much older, you can guess what was often said: "Oh, she was a booboo...a change of life baby...an oops." The last one is the one I remember most. Oh, I know when people say those things they don't realize it hurts. But once said, you can't take it back. Some forty years later I shared those names with my sisters and they were appalled. "Mother and daddy were thrilled when they learned they were expecting!" Maybe so, but I was still an "unexpected" child. They told me stories of how spoiled I was in my early years, how even my brother carried my baby picture in his wallet when he joined

3

the military. Be that as it may, that was *their* remembrance, not mine.

Truth is that perception is more important than reality. In fact, perception *is* reality for the perceiver. What I experienced wasn't what they remembered. My reality was totally different, and if I had to choose one adjective to describe the early part of my life, the word would be "lonely."

The house where we lived was at the top of a hill. Nobody came to our house when it was snowing because many times the hill was so slippery, people were afraid they would slide down the hill before they could turn into the driveway!   I was told that the lot on which our house was built used to be part of the town dump. Before I was born my father had purchased it along with the land below the hill. Years later the extra area would be where my father raised hundreds of chickens and turkeys, and still later, the land was divided up into house lots that ended up becoming wedding presents to my brother and my older sister, with the other sister purchasing her lot some time later. But when I was born, most of the land was vacant.

My father drove a school bus and he had a dump truck and both were stored below the hill. Adding to my sisters' perception of how my parents felt about my birth, the dump truck had a name: Betty Ann! But I was too young to remember; this was simply information from a photograph.

My mother and me

4

Grandpa Lane & my father

1950 – 2 years old

Christmas 1950

1951 – 3 years old

My first real memory came the Christmas before I turned five, 1952. My mother had just become a grandmother on Halloween of that year; she was the youngest grandmother among all her friends...just 41 years old. True to the memories of everyone else, that Christmas was like any other; I received more presents than any one child should. There is even an 8mm film of Christmas morning when I was surveying all the gifts under the tree, eyeing one gift in particular: a doll carriage. And it wasn't like the doll carriages of today. It actually looked like it could have been a *real* baby carriage—a pram— and I had placed a baby doll in it, covered her ever so perfectly, and stood there proudly, looking

5

over what I had done. What happened next was the beginning of a formation that would stay with me the rest of my life.

My brother's wife came into the room holding my mother's new grandson. The lights on the Christmas tree paled in comparison to the look on my mother's face as she beheld this little child. Now that *I'm* a grandmother, I get it. I understand exactly what it must have been like for my mother because I remember the day I held my first grandson in my arms. The world stood still and I would have moved mountains and walked on broken glass if that had been a requirement to be a grandmother. But at almost-five-years old, such thoughts were nowhere to be had.

As the movie camera clicked on and the scene became a little chaotic, my mother, although unaware, altered my self-worth in just a few seconds. With a one-handed, sweeping motion, she reached into the doll carriage, removed the carefully placed blanket and baby doll, and replaced them with her new grandson! I stood there with my hands on my hips like a little, spoiled brat. I surveyed what had just happened to something that I was so proud of...something that was so important to me, and I ran out of the room...the camera still rolling on the otherwise happy family. Years later I was to learn about a similar incident that occurred with my grandson and his father. To his mother's credit—bless her heart—she spoke to her son, assured him that what had just happened to discredit his feelings was wrong, and that he was loved.

Children are so vulnerable, especially in the first five or six years of their life. Parents are supposed to be a child's safe place to fall. That's not what happened on that Christmas Day in 1952. The rest of the day brings up no memories, but the message was clear: *You aren't important. Your feelings don't matter.* That message stayed with me, in varying degrees, for over 50 years. My message to you? Be careful how you treat little ones; you are building the foundation that will follow them the rest of their lives. First and foremost, make sure they are grounded in love.

By the time I started school, I might as well have been an only child. My closest sibling was almost eighteen, and those early memories are sporadic at best. Below the hill from our house, we had chickens, laying hens and turkeys….lots of them! There was a building behind our house that had a large walk-in cooler, lots of counter space and cabinets…a lot like an over-sized kitchen. Beside the chicken pens there was a building that was lovingly called "the killing house." It was where my father would take the chickens and turkeys, hang them by one foot, and slit their throats to drain out all the blood. Then he would put them in scalding water, hang them up again, pluck out all their feathers and somehow get them ready for packaging to sell.

A Christmas angel 2nd grade   *An Annie Oakley wanna-be*

I may have the order of events *out* of order, but you get the picture. We raised chickens to kill and sell. I chuckle about that today…me, who takes care of my fingernails along with getting a pedicure every three weeks spent a couple of memorable summers in the killing house plucking chicken feathers with my father! Go figure.

When the chickens and turkeys were cooked, the meat was boned out and my mother made little individual chicken and turkey pies to sell. The building with the walk-in cooler became a retail store and people from all over town came for Lane's Chicken Pies and 3½ pound chickens. This was a big deal in a little town in the early 50's.

In hindsight, the time I spent with my father in the killing house, was probably the closest I ever felt to him. I remember some laughter and I remember his smile. He enjoyed what he did. And he may have even enjoyed the time we spent together. I can only hope.

7

Even though my school was a short walk from the house, my oldest sister drove me almost every day. She had married when I was four years old and she and her husband built a house across the street from us. I remember that many of my friends thought she was my mother because she was 20 years older than me, closer to the ages of their mothers. She certainly wasn't taken for my sister!

One destiny that was unescapable for me was piano lessons. It was a fate worse than death, and what I didn't know at the time was there was no way I would be allowed to quit if I wanted to. You see, after two years of lessons, both my sisters had quit and later, they were sorry. So when I came along, brandishing two hands with ten fingers, my goose was cooked. I would spend the next eleven years taking lessons from two different nuns, sometimes happy doing it but mostly annoyed and disliking it. In the early years I often didn't practice, thinking that my mother would get tired of paying money for lessons while listening to an annoyed nun chastise me for not practicing. It didn't work. The nun tried to make me feel bad and I got in trouble with my mother on the way home from every lesson. Yet, even in this early time of my life, I was developing a talent that would be one day lead a secondary career, not to mention a life-saver. God is always working, even when we might be too young to follow directions!

 For the first six years my mother would wait across the hall in the sitting room in the convent while I had my lesson. My love/hate relationship with the piano continued for many years. It wasn't until I taught myself how to play the organ and it got me a fill-in church organist job that I realized I was lucky that I hadn't quit my lessons. And it wasn't until I was an adult that I realized just how important this musical gift was or would be in my life. I guess that's one good thing that I can thank my mother for...

At some point my parents' retail business began to grow bigger than the little building behind our house could handle. Besides, in the winter, people were afraid to come to the house because of the hill. Many a car had slide down that hill during a snowstorm. So my father secured a small building on the main road. He phased out the chicken and turkey farm, purchased the product wholesale, bought two large barbeque machines and started another business: Lane's Bar-B-Q. He had a secret recipe for soaking the chickens before putting them on the barbeque spits. Again, like the chicken pies, it was a hit. A 3½ lb. barbequed chicken...$1.79! Daily he cooked hundreds of them, especially toward the end of the week. That's about the time I became a "latch key kid". Didn't learn that term for many years, but that's what I was. I think I was about seven. The store was right up the street from my school and just a block away from where we lived, so if I got tired of sitting in the back of the store after school, I could just walk home. I had a key.

Not too long after that my father built a restaurant across the main road on the next block. Barbeque customers planted the idea in my father's head that a restaurant would be a great idea...a place to *eat* the chicken instead of taking it home. There were no local restaurants in our small town, so the time was right...for a restaurant, that is, not for me. I stopped at the restaurant after school before I walked home. Sometimes I even walked to the restaurant for lunch. (You could do that then!) I was the envy of all my friends! Imagine, being able to go to a restaurant every noon and every night and choose FROM A MENU what you wanted to eat! Wow! Any of them would have changed places with me in a heartbeat. That would certainly have been better than going home to a mother with cookies and milk on the table, asking questions about his or her day! Little did they know how much I would have preferred the cookies and conversation...if not the milk...

> *"And we know that in all things*
> *God works for the good of those*
> *who love Him, who have been called*
> *according to His purpose."*
> Romans 8:28

My grammar school education at Holy Ghost School was perhaps the best in some areas, but not so good in others. I was one of 30 children in one classroom, all day for nine years (which included kindergarten!) Imagine, the same kids for nine years. I only remember one kid leaving and one kid coming in 7th grade. Crazy! I had nuns for seven of those years, and two lay teachers: Mrs. Fitzgerald in 3rd grade and Mrs. Maurano in 7th grade. A few things stand out in those nine years: sitting under Mrs. Fitzgerald's keyhole desk for a half day with my gum pressed onto my forehead; Sr. Anthony Margaret, my 4th grade teacher, with whom I have two painful memories; boys!; breaking a little first-grader's glasses while playing "whip"; a book called Three Crowns for Elizabeth; meeting Fr. Christopher Davis; and, did I mention 'boys'!?

Thinking about these things is amazingly vivid. Classrooms in those days was pretty depressing...nothing like the decorative, colorful room of today's grammar schools. Holy Ghost School was a small, Catholic school that survived on individual tuition, and if I remember correctly, it was $35 a month, certainly a lot in those days. The classrooms consisted of dark, worn wooden desks, chairs attached, all lined up in a row on a floor of non-descript tile...a blackboard that took up the entire front wall, above which hung penmanship cards, left to right, showing us the alphabet in cursive. Mrs. Fitzgerald was an older woman (so I thought then, but she was probably no more than 50!) And you didn't mess with her! One day she caught me chewing gum and she made me put it on my forehead and sit on the floor under her big old keyhole desk for most of the day!

In fourth grade I met Sr. Anthony Margaret, and oh, I just loved her, and that's probably why the events that happened with her were so upsetting. The first had to do with a book entitled Hail Mary, Full of Grace. For some reason it had come in the mail and, being a good Roman Catholic, I had a special devotion to Mary, so I thought this would be such a special book. The day after it came in the mail, I brought it to school to show Sister. I was so proud and I wanted her to be proud of me, being interested in such a book. I remember vividly... *"Sister, Sister, look at my new book!"* I came running across the playground just before the morning bell rang. She took the book and looked at it. Opening the front cover, she read the small print. Surprisingly, she looked sternly at me and promptly kept the book! She said I wasn't allowed to read it because it wasn't an approved publication. Much later when I was old enough to question and understand what she meant, I learned that Catholics weren't allowed to read

10

any religious book that didn't have *nihil obstat* and *Imprimatur*, stamped on the inside. Both are Latin words, followed by a bishop's or cardinal's name. The first meant "No obstacle"; the second, a bishop's seal...both assuring the reader that there was nothing in the book that was against the teaching of the Catholic Church.

Surely, Sister was simply following the rules, but again, at what price? My book was gone, and the nun that I loved dearly had hurt me. I didn't understand and a person I had held close drifted away.

> "Have I not commanded you?
>
> Be strong and courageous.
>
> Do not be afraid...or discouraged, for the Lord your
>
> God will be with you wherever you go."
>
> Joshua 1:9

In the fifties, we actually had recess. There was a large blacktop area between the school and the church. At least one nun would walk up and down the playground, directly in the middle of the area—the boys were on one side and the girls were on the other. Most of the boys could have cared less about the girls, but the girls? Well, that's a different story... especially me! Any time I could sneak onto the boy's side of the playground, I did. I don't know why, really. Perhaps they knew something we didn't. Turns out they did have a lot of misinformation about lots of things, like where babies came from and the difference between girl and boy body parts. Sometimes I wonder how I ever grew up with all my wits about me!

When I wasn't trying to sneak onto the boy's side of the playground, I was playing "whip." It was a game we really weren't allowed to play because someone could get hurt, but we did it anyway. A bunch of kids would hold hands and run. The leader in the line would run in a straight-line at first, then they would zig-zag across the playground, eventually "whipping" everybody around, back and forth. The farther back you were in the line, the harder it was to keep up. Eventually you were pulled

11

faster than your feet could carry you. Those in the back would end up falling down or crashing into something. And on this particular day, I was the one who crashed, right into a little first-grade girl who was wearing glasses. We both fell and her glasses broke. Once again Sr. Anthony Margaret was the nun who hauled me into the principal's office. But here's the thing about this story: it was bad enough what happened, but as the accident was unfolding, I had a little bit of control over where I fell—it was either on top of the little girl with the glasses or crash into Sr. Anthony Margaret! As I could see the crisis unfolding, I knew deep down that if I crashed into a nun, I would immediately get struck by lightning or go directly to hell or something much worse—if that was possible. You see, nuns and priests were special. They were *so far* above real people that they were like God Himself. So they couldn't be touched, not even by accident. The little girl with the glasses? Well, it was a no brainer. How pathetic is that?! Obviously I was still in my impressionable years and I was getting all the *wrong* impressions about people who were called by God to do his work.

Somewhere during my grammar school years I came across a book in our little library called Three Crowns for Elizabeth. Our library, the size of a small kitchen, contained only religious books about saints, and the only reason this book attracted my attention was because it had my name in it! This was the start of a fascination for the saints, especially those who gave up everything to follow Jesus, some even giving up their lives. This book, written for nine to fifteen year olds, is about Saint Elizabeth of Hungary who spent her life quite differently than most saints. Instead of living in poverty like St. Francis of Assisi, for example, she was born Princess Elizabeth of Hungary, living most of her life in a castle surrounded by incredible wealth. By the age of four she was already engaged to be married and was sent far away from her home to live with Louis, her husband-to-be, who was only 10 years old. People ridiculed Elizabeth because they noticed that she was always trying to be holy. She always wanted to sneak into the chapel and visit with Jesus. Her love of God and her growing understanding of the poverty in other people made her become a member of the Third Order of St. Francis and she constantly gave away her riches to the poor. Only four years after her death she was canonized a saint. Her three crowns? The crown of royalty, the crown of poverty, and the crown of sainthood. It was a fascinating story, the kind of a story that drew me into the concept of closeness to God and living a life that would please him. A seed was planted that would take many decades to produce the necessary fruit that would lead me to my life's goal...

Some time after I had written the bulk of this book and I was proof-reading it, I realized that I had forgotten something that occurred in fourth grade, again with Sr. Anthony Margaret, that warped my understanding of the love of God...and that misunderstanding lasted until way into adulthood. It was Lent, and Sister had hung a picture of a crown of thorns on the wall. The picture was probably three or four feet square, so the thorns where huge. About a week before Lent started, Sister gave us our Lenten "challenge.". On her desk was a pad of rosebud stickers. And the challenge was this: if we got up early every school day and attended 7am Mass, we would be allowed to take a rosebud from the sticker book and place it on one of the thorns. Obviously the plan was to cover all the thorns by Easter. And the opposite unspoken result? *Not* attending Mass was contributing to Jesus' pain! Nobody said it, but the mind of a fourth grader runs wild. The moral of the story? Again, children are vulnerable, and children are important; make sure that the foundation of every message is clearly love. If you don't do that, children will create their own message, and chances are, it will be wrong and difficult to correct...if ever.

> *Now faith is the assurance*
> *of things hoped for, the conviction*
> *of things not seen.*
> Hebrews 11:1

You've heard the expression: Some people come into your life for a reason, a season or for a lifetime? Well, Fr. Christopher Davis was surely sent from God...for a lifetime. He actually came to my ordination forty years later. But I'm getting ahead of myself...

He came into my life when I was twelve. He was a Benedictine priest and monk who lived at the Portsmouth Priory. He was assigned to Holy Ghost Church on Sundays to help with extra

Masses. What I remember about him began to turn the tide of my feelings about myself...and God. He was kind, always had time to listen to me, and I was so taken by his countenance. He always had a smile on his face. Why, I didn't know, but whatever he had, I wanted it! I remember his sermons were always about the lives of the saints. Perhaps that's why the fascination grew...all these ancient people who loved God so much they gave up everything and followed Him. And they were happy, no matter what happened to them. I wanted that! Little did I know...

Somewhere in these early grammar school years a spark was lit. I can't put my finger on it. God was always there but I didn't get it. There was, however, that time when I set up an altar of sorts in my upstairs bedroom! I took a piece of bread, flattened it out and cut a "host" using an upside down glass like a biscuit cutter. Then there was the glass I used for the chalice. It looked like a little goblet that came with some kind of Cheese Whiz in it from the grocery store. I made a friend of mine function as an altar boy (and she was a girl), and I "said Mass." Okay, I was a little strange. But was that a sign of the future?

And then there were the times when I wanted to look at my sister's coffee table Bible. In those days everybody had a large family Bible on the coffee table. In it would be recorded important dates like baptisms, First Communions, marriages, births and deaths. Did anyone open it up to read it? Certainly not. It was a book to be honored, not touched. Where did we get such an idea? But apparently, that didn't stop me. Taking a deep breath, I remember asking my sister if I could look at it. She took great pains to sit me on the couch, smooth out my dress, put the book on my lap and show me how to turn the pages so as to not tear or wrinkle them. I'm sure if she saw my seminary Bible, she would have had a stroke at all the markings and highlighting in it! I was too little to read the words, but the pictures...oh, the pictures. In my minds eye, I can still see them, especially the Scourging at the Pillar: Jesus tied to a post, practically naked, looking up to heaven, deep gashes across his back. Why did that picture strike me above all the others? The inhumanity of the act? Perhaps. But as a little girl who really hadn't yet grasped my salvation, I think it was more about me. Jesus was hurting and alone; so was I.

In September 1961 I began my four years at Mt. St. Mary Academy in Fall River, Massachusetts. There was no high school in Tiverton, so the town bussed us to Fall River where we had several choices of parochial schools and one public school. I'm not sure how I chose "The Mount" as we called it, but it was a very interesting four years, to say the least. An all- girls academy, I thrived on the religious studies and retreats while learning that nothing good could come from a relationship with a teenage boy. Yet, the point of our education was to graduate, get married and populate the world!

Some girls did go to college and become teachers or nurses, but the rest of us learned typing, shorthand, bookkeeping, and got married. There was no helpful preparation for the real world and the older I got, the more I sought attention from the opposite sex. Looking back on it now I was more of a loner than a groupy. I had a couple of close friends, but not really close. It wasn't a great experience—it just *was*... I did what I was supposed to do, didn't ruffle any feathers, except to roll my skirt up to make it look shorter, and roll my knee socks down to resemble bobbie socks. That was about the extent of my "bad behavior."

As I look back on it all—thirteen years of school—I think about the place I called home: 172 West Hooper Street. There is an occasional memory of one or two things, but what I remember most is being alone. It's just the way it was; it was sad, and all these years later, the word that comes to mind is *apathetic*. There was one bright spot, though. Rushing home after school to watch *American Bandstand* on television, dreaming of being one of those lucky girls who had a boyfriend. Other than that, I opened up a can of something for dinner or walked up the street to the restaurant. But as I got older, I think I began to realize what I'd missed, and I looked for a replacement: boys!

I had a few boyfriends in high school, nothing really serious. Being able to say you had a "boyfriend" meant you had talked on the phone a time or two and you might get a glimpse of each other on the street or at a basketball game. That was about it. But I could certainly fantasize about what having a *real* boyfriend would be like.

15

I've heard many stories of high school days where life-long friendships were forged, memories abounded, and fun accompanied learning. I don't have those memories. First of all, it was an all-girls Catholic academy where the worse thing I did was roll up my skirt and roll down my knee socks. While other girls teased their hair, which got them a visit to the principal's office, I was concerned about getting to class on time: single file, down the left of the corridor, with nuns watching from every classroom. I walked so close to the right side of the corridor that I was always banging my right elbow on the locker handles!

I made a couple of friends but I guess I was too straight laced and it showed. I wasn't going to try anything that wasn't permitted. I did, however, want to join the glee club, but practices were after school and I had to take a bus, so that wasn't an option. Having to take a bus also meant that no after school activities were available to me. Perhaps the drama club might have gotten me out of my shell, but it didn't happen. One time I remember had to do with Anne O'Connell, Janice Gagne and Cheryl Rodrigues. We had gone to grammar school together. Cheryl had her driver's license and had access to a car! We went "cruising" one night. My mother thought I was at "play practice." I didn't sleep for days thinking she would find out. And all we did was drive in and out of a MacDonald's, looking for boys. No alcohol or drugs were involved. Oh, those were the days!

In my sophomore year, John F. Kennedy was shot; November 22, 1963. We had finished classes for the day and were returning to our homerooms. It was about 1:35pm. I remember whispering in the hallways which was unheard of, and the watching nuns weren't stopping it. We were told about the shooting when we were all seated. I'm not sure I fully understood because the first thing that crossed my mind was really awful: *If the president was shot, maybe there won't be a dance at the fire barn tomorrow night!* What can I say? I was a teenager with one thing on my mind.

Our school dances were nothing like the programs you see on television today. As I think about it, I'm amazed that we could get *any* boys to accompany us to those dances. Why do I say that? Well, the dances were in the school auditorium and at least a half-

16

dozen nuns lined the vestibule to inspect our attire and to be introduced to every boy that came through the door! Our dates were in suits and ties and we were in long or short dresses, depending on the dance. I always wondered how it was that boys were acceptable at school dances, but they'd better not show up at any *other* time during the school year! If a boy was going to drop you off in the morning for school, he'd better do it a block away. Oh, to have those days back again…not!

I met Mike in grammar school. He was a year ahead of me. He was tall and handsome and, at that time, that was all I needed to capture my attention. Thinking about it now, there was surely something else: he had a mother at home that I could visit. They lived right across the street from Lane's Bar-B-Q on the main road in Tiverton. (This was my father's first business before the restaurant.) The church and the school were just down the street from Lane's, and a block away from our house. Very convenient. I liked his mother and it gave me the excuse of getting to see Mike, even if he didn't seem to be interested in me. He had a little brother that was sometimes in a highchair, and it was fun sitting with his mother and little Kevin.

Jr. Prom - 1964
(This was taken at my parents' restaurant: Lane's Restaurant. The guy's name? I don't remember! He and his family used to come to restaurant. I waited on them and I thought he was cute, so I invited him to the Jr. Prom! Crazy!)

The Roberts' family moved to Portsmouth at some point and Mike ended up going to DeLaSalle Academy in Newport while I headed to high school in Fall River. I can't remember how we stayed in touch or how we saw each other. One of the things I do remember

17

is that sometimes he would "thumb" to Tiverton to see me. Eventually he was able to take his dad's car, but he had to be home by ten because his mother worked as a waitress at the Officer's Club in Newport and his dad had to pick her up. She didn't drive. Somehow we ended up getting engaged. (That sentence is crazy...how do you *not know* how you got engaged? It just happened.)

At that time my father had bought the piece of property on the next block from Mike's parent's house on the main road and opened a restaurant. He built sort of a little apartment in the basement of the restaurant, like a home away from home. I think it was to be a place for me after school so I wouldn't always have to go home by myself, particularly since the restaurant stayed open later at night than the bar-b-q that was across the street.

I remember Mike and I spending some time in that little "apartment". We must have gotten to know each other a little; perhaps we even kissed.

After the senior prom – 1965
(We didn't go out and party.
we came home and had cake
with my parents!)

High School graduation 1965

We became engaged in that very room. I actually think we talked about it and I was the one who initiated it. I even asked him to get down on one knee, which he did reluctantly. Crazy! I was 18 and he was 19. Little did I know that this was yet again another part of God's plan.

18

Much later I learned that both our parents thought we were nuts, but interestingly enough, no one ever said it to our faces, not that it would have probably made a difference. I can't speak for him, but this was going to be my fairytale experience: a husband, a family, the rose-covered cottage, and we would live happily ever after. Nobody told me those chances are few and far between. And at that time, we never even talked about *where* that rose-covered cottage would be!

I have very small glimpses of my mother growing up. Apathy isn't a feeling that you would connect with a mother-daughter relationship, but it's the only word that comes to mind. When I was born the family was well established and I wanted for nothing, unlike my sisters and brother. I remember hearing stories of orange crates for kitchen chairs and having a formal portrait of my sister and brother repossessed because my parents couldn't pay for it. Hardships like that often bind a family together. Such hardship didn't exist when I was born. Maybe that's why my mother and I were disconnected. She had already been through twenty years of marriage that had its difficult times. The hurdles had been cleared. Another child wasn't in her plan I'm sure.

As I search for memories, the first one that comes to mind is her mastectomy. I was sixteen. The day of her surgery her hospital room was like a circus. It's a good thing the room was extremely large. I remember thinking I'd never seen a hospital room that large, but we managed to fill it up! Besides the immediate family, four of her sisters were going in and out of the room, waiting for word of the surgery. And as if that wasn't enough confusion, my thirty-five-year old brother was across the hall, having just had a circumcision. Go figure!

In the sixties, no one said the word "cancer." It was called "The Big C." My mother had discovered a large black and blue mark on her left breast near her armpit. She didn't pay much attention to it at the time, and I guess someone called it to her attention. A

19

doctor visit happened, and the rest is history. Truth be known, no one actually told me she had cancer. I sort of learned it from all the whispering I'd heard for many months. I guess they all thought I wasn't old enough to know what was going on, so they simply didn't tell me anything. Funny how I remember walking around that room, looking at all the long faces as they commiserated with one another, seeing my brother limping into the room from time to time. It was as if I was outside myself looking at all these people, but they didn't see me. It was very strange...and sad to think about at this point in time.

When they wheeled my mother into the room, I vividly remember what I saw. She was a full-figured woman before the surgery. Now, the left side of the sheet was flush with her shoulder. Something was clearly missing. It was her left breast. Before she went into surgery, I only knew that she had "the big C." I knew nothing of the possibility of a mastectomy. I'd never even heard the word. Her sisters were distraught. *My* sisters were trying to keep it together. And me? I was still watching the whole thing from another level. It was a family crisis, and I was on the outside looking in. It was no one's fault. That's just the way it was.

Weeks later I accidently walked by the bathroom when my mother was doing her exercises. She had to stand close to a wall and creep *up* the wall with the fingers on her left hand. I learned later that this was to help her stretch and strengthen her arm. The higher she could extend the "creeping," the sooner she would heal. Then I saw it. It was only a second or two, but I'll never forget it. This type of surgery was brutal in the sixties. My mother's incision went from above her naval, through where her left breast was, through her armpit and halfway to her elbow. (I just stopped writing to take a measurement on myself: it was about 17 inches...the most barbaric thing I had ever seen. I don't know if she saw me. Surely she would have been mortified. I quickly walked on to where I was going. Not having had a relationship up until this point, this certainly wasn't exactly a bonding opportunity. She never complained, at least not that I know of. But we were like strangers in the same house. Sad but true. That was one of the times I had said to myself, "If I ever had children, I will *never* treat them the way I was treated!" Words thought of, if not spoken, by a teenager in emotional pain. My mother was hurting too, but she didn't know how to bring me in. The surgery bought her five more years. The cancer returned...bones, blood, and finally brain. She was sixty-one years old. So much was unsaid, missed. Some children are smarter than their parents realize.

20

I've said a few things about my mother, so I guess it's only fair to mention my father. Notice that I've said "mother" and "father", not "mom" or "dad." I never knew why that was so until a counseling session I had in seminary. It was solidified when Joel and I married. It was then I saw what that kind of relationship should look like. When Joel speaks of his mother and father, he always says "my mom" and "my dad." I've come to understand "mom" and "dad" are saved for those who had a relationship with that parent. Those endearing terms can't even pass my lips to this day. But I digress...

Every little girl wants a relationship with her father. A father is a protector, a guide, someone a daughter can look up to. I didn't have any of that and I don't know why. I guess it has to come from the parent, and while I had everything I could have ever wanted, it wasn't what I needed. When the Father-Daughter Dance came around in high school, I thought long and hard about telling my father about it. Could he even dance? More importantly, could we spend a whole evening together? What would we talk about? Would he even want to go? I sucked it up one afternoon and asked him. He said yes and I was glad.

I vaguely remember a few smiles on the dance floor of the auditorium and he *could* dance! But we hardly talked at all. After the dance we went to a nearby diner for a soda. Remember the vintage diners where you sat at the counter on round stools and waitresses were all dressed alike? That's where we were. I remember us sitting at the counter. I asked if he had had a good time and he said yes. That's all I remember. Nothing else. We drove home. He was a nice man but that's not the description I always wanted of my father. He gave me everything. I wanted for nothing. He did compliment me on the way I ran the outgoing customer orders at the restaurant, especially when I was expecting my first child. I could barely get behind the cash register when it was open, but I could wait on a dozen people at a time and not make one mistake. He said nobody did a better job. I suppose I was grateful for the compliment. But I wanted more...

As I write this, I try to remember what Mike and I had, what brought us together, what we expected to find in each other. I have no answers to those questions. Neither of us were ready for such a commitment. Did we love each other? As much as two kids could at that age, I guess, but I don't really know. Being old enough to secure a marriage license isn't enough, and the poor excuse for premarital counseling that we had...well, that's another story.

On April 23, 1966, Mike and I were married in Holy Ghost Church. And the *real* world began...

April 23, 1966
Holy Ghost Church,
Tiverton, RI

CHAPTER 2

159 West Hooper Street
Tiverton, Rhode Island

> A ranch house, bluish-gray, two-bedrooms, one bath, a screened-in porch on the back of the house, a big back yard, a lilac bush in the front, beautiful in the spring

Moving into this house wasn't a big change for me. I'd been in this house many times since I was four years old. My oldest sister built this house when she and her husband were married in 1952. She began her family in this house and I was her babysitter. But this house was more than that to me. Since I spent a lot of time alone after school, I enjoyed being with my sister and her children, and it was a short walk...just across the street! More importantly, it felt like a family.

Eventually, my sister's family out grew this house and needed to move. I was young, engaged and clueless about a lot of things, including what was happening right under my nose. While my sister was having a four-bedroom, split-level house built across the street where my father used to raise his chickens and turkeys, he was now planning to buy Ella's first house with the intention of renting it to Mike and me. As I think about it now, my mother was planning a wedding that she didn't really think was a good idea and we had no thought to where we were going to live! Hindsight is an amazing thing, isn't it? As I dredge up memories long since forgotten or buried, I realize how foolish we were. Ah, but God had a plan, and I'll get to that in a minute... You see, God was still very present with me, even though I didn't know it. There's an old saying, "If you feel distant from God, guess who moved?" How true that is! I didn't realize how important it would be for God to be the third person in my marriage. Nevertheless, success or failure, he would be there.

A weekend train trip to New York City—that was our honeymoon. I so wish I had some memories of that honeymoon...what we did, what we ate, where we went. But I can raise none, except for one. In retrospect, it used to be funny when I thought about it, but when I got older I realized it was simply sad. Our wedding night left much to be desired. We were both virgins. Suffice it to say that we knew nothing about what a wedding night should be like. Having said that, it was the most painful, physical experience I ever had. Remember, earlier I mentioned that pre-marital counseling left something to be desired? Well, on the night we supposed to be hearing about sex from a doctor, that doctor had been called away to deliver a baby! We were left there looking at each other with no plan to bring us back to perhaps learn something that would be incredibly important to a married couple. The following morning in St. Patrick's Cathedral, I was in so much pain that I practically had to stand up through the entire service! We were just trying to fulfill our duty, which of course would be to "populate the world with a lot of little Catholics." And it was awful! I don't know whether I heard that phrase somewhere or if I just felt that way because of the way the nuns taught us. What was so confusing was the mixed messages we received. During high school we were supposed to stay away from boys—sex was never a topic of discussion...and yet, when we graduated we were supposed to get married and have babies.... No wonder things worked out the way they did.

Someone once said that if you have a good sex life, it's only ten percent of your marriage, but if you don't have a good sex life, it's ninety percent of your marriage. I guess we started with handicap. But regardless of that part of the marriage that wasn't like a fairytale, it didn't take me long to "nest." It was so much fun, outfitting a home where I hoped to be happy with my husband and create a family. I was working at Raytheon Submarine Signal Division, in Portsmouth, making about $60 a week. Mike was working part time at the local grocery store making about $20 a week while going to Rhode Island Junior College for journalism. It was 1966.

I don't remember the cost of living, but I do remember the "lay-away" plan. I used it a lot! Whether it was at a department store, a furniture store or just a simple, white envelope in the desk drawer, it took some time to purchase just about anything. The living room set was the biggest purchase: a sofa bed, two side chairs, a coffee table, two end tables, two lamps, and a braided rug: $175! I remember saving $5 a week for seven weeks to buy a vacuum cleaner. And the rent? $75 a month! Wouldn't it be great to go back to *those* prices!

24

Perhaps the most important decision I ever made during the first year of our marriage...maybe in my *life*... was to make an appointment with a gynecologist in Newport. We were married about six months and I wasn't pregnant; to me, that meant something was wrong. Most of my friends at work thought I was crazy for wanting to be pregnant, given the amount of money that my husband and I were bringing home a week. Be that as it may, I saw the doctor, and I was right. There was something wrong: ovarian cysts, one the size of an orange, the other the size of a grapefruit encircling the ovary and the fallopian tube. Immediate surgery was necessary. And the only thing I could think of was, "Am I going to lose my job?" It never occurred to me to wonder if I would be able to have children when all this was over. How naïve! But in hindsight, I had the trust of a child...something Jesus talked about all the time. The doctor was going to fix me and I'd be able to start my family. And that's exactly what happened. On Election Day, 1966, I had surgery. My recovery time was approximately six weeks. I could return to "normal" the second week of December. And on September 13, 1967, Lisa was born. Trust is a wonderful thing... And 15 months later, Christopher was born.

There was a point when my father told me that we should *buy* the house from him because the mortgage wouldn't cost that much more and it would be ours. He was right. Our mortgage ended up costing $95 a month. Can you believe that? Imagine, owning our own home at the ripe old age of 20!

You know, when I started this writing project I thought I would remember lots of things, but the truth is that the farther back I go, my memories are only of those things that hurt. It's sad to think that happy memories are seldom to be found.

> *What no eye has seen, nor ear heard,*
> *nor the human heart conceived,*
> *What God has prepared*
> *for those who love him.*
> 1 Cor. 2:9

The first couple of years of marriage were non-descript. Mike was a lineman and worked away from home sometimes, especially during winter storms. I was home with the two children, enjoying every moment with them. But my cluelessness continued.

One Saturday he told me that he was going to help a friend move. So off he went fairly early in the morning. As the day grew into late afternoon, I began to wonder when he would be coming home. So I called his friend to see if the moving was close to completion. The guy's mother answered the phone and she said that her son was home and had been there all day...and, by the way, he wasn't moving! Lisa was about three as I recall and I remember her awareness of her mommy being upset. She hovered around me as if she knew something was wrong. Around dinnertime, Mike appeared at the door. He was barely inside when I screamed, "Where have you been? And don't tell me about moving your friend because I talked to his mother and he isn't moving!" He looked at me with a dazed expression and told me that he had met another woman and he was leaving me! I'm not sure exactly what I said or did at that point, I just remember thinking: *what will I do with two children? I don't have a job, and how will I get along?* I think I voiced that through tears and sobs at some point, and he said that he'd break it off and stay. I don't even remember being relieved. Surely I needed more.

The next few weeks were difficult, to say the least. We hardly talked about the issue and I assumed he had done what he said he was going to do. Then one day, as I was going over a telephone bill, I noticed consistent collect calls to our number on Tuesday evenings. That was my bowling night. I got up the courage to call the number and learned it was the other woman. Apparently, he hadn't broken it off at all, and I will never forget what she said to me: "You may have his body, but I have his heart!" When Mike came home from work that night, I told him about the phone bill and my phone call. Once again he said he would break it off.

In hindsight, I realize that I spent the next seven years in denial of the reality that I didn't have a marriage at all, in the true sense of the word. But early on there was one amazing event that to this day I still don't understand. Perhaps it was the one chance we had at making our marriage work that we didn't grasp; perhaps it was a glimpse of what marriage really should be. Whatever it was, I never forgot it. And to this day, I wonder...

26

We took a motorcycle vacation to Cape Cod. Lisa stayed with Aunt Cynthia and Christopher stayed with Grandma and Grandpa Roberts. Off we went, a huge knapsack on my back along with other things attached somehow to the back of the bike! We had little money and had made no reservations for a place to stay when we arrived. It was late when we pulled into a campground of sorts. We didn't need much space with just a bike, so we pulled up between a couple of trees on a little incline. Mike covered the bike with a tarp that he had brought, we set up the sleeping bag...on the hill, by the way...and we bedded down for the night. I remember us looking at each other and laughing...about what, I don't know, but for the very first time—and it never happened again—there was something like a closeness between us. And then it started to rain! As the water ran down the hill, it got into the sleeping bag, complete with dirt and mud. The morning couldn't have come any too soon for me. When the sun rose we discovered that there was a large public building not more than twenty feet away where we could have gotten out of the rain. At the very least I tried to wash some of the mud out of the sleeping bag ...and my hair! Everything was wet when we repacked the bike, and it was twice as heavy! What a spectacle we were, I'm sure.

The trip was short-lived because the children weren't doing well without us. They did a lot of crying. In hindsight, separating them probably wasn't the best idea. But I wasn't thinking of them at the time; I was thinking of my marriage. And for a fleeting moment, maybe it *was* a marriage...

Love is patient, love is kind...
It bears all things, believes all things,
hopes all things, endures all things...
1 Cor. 13:4, 7

CHAPTER 3

102 Beechwood Drive
Westport, Massachusetts

> A large ranch house with a garage, three bedrooms, one bath, a big kitchen, a big yard, within walking distance of a lake, a nice neighborhood.

"I'm glad mother didn't live to see you move away!" My sister Maureen said that when we bought the house in Westport. It was nine miles away! Funny as it sounds, she believed this really was an issue. You see, all of us didn't just live in the same town. At some point, we all lived on the same street: five houses of parents and four married children. My mother had died around this time and I was in my third pregnancy. A two-bedroom house would no longer suffice. So we found a nice place in a nice neighborhood — in another town — in another state — nine miles away!

You may have noticed that this is only the second time I've mentioned my mother. I've had to dig deep to find memories that could be shared, and there are precious few. Let's see…there are scattered memories of all of us sitting at the table, food almost completely eaten before my mother sat down with us; the time I was in the kitchen with her and I asked her why my father didn't go to church with us (and her answer always amazed me: "Oh, he's too old for that…" I didn't ask her what that meant.) Then there was the time I mentioned earlier when she had her mastectomy.

It's so sad to not be able to share your feelings with someone you're supposed to love. I thank God every day that after some forty years of hoping and praying, I have found someone with whom I can be honest, and it is a gift beyond compare.

> *A friend loves at all times, and*
> *kinsfolk are born to share adversity.*
> Proverbs 17:17

The day before my mother died, my sisters and I went shopping for our black dresses! Oh, my, how awful that sounds today, but I guess that was a way of coping with what was to come. My mother had been at home in a hospital bed for a time, my father taking care of her. He ended up selling the restaurant in order to spend more time with her. The doctors couldn't take care of her pain with conventional drugs anymore, so the day before she died, they gave her one dose of something called Cobraxon. We were told that it was the venom from a cobra. Once you receive this toxin, there's no turning back. If the medical community had miraculously found a cure for cancer that afternoon, it would have been too late for my mother. That's how powerful the drug was. She only received one dose. She died that night. I remember I was sitting in the living room of my home across the street, shortening the hem on my new black dress. My sister came to the front door. "She's gone," was the message, and I went back to hemming my dress. My husband was asleep and I was alone in the living room. There was no outburst of grief like I heard from my father the next day at the kitchen table. There was no moment of sadness. There was just...nothing. At the cemetery I remember looking at the cement cover, standing up against some sort of device that would lower the cover onto the cement vault after we all left. Etched in the concrete cover was a large lily and inscribed with the lily was her name and the appropriate dates. I should have felt something. I should have felt a sense of loss; after all, it was my mother. But I didn't. It was time to go... to move on and watch other people grieve... And it was shortly thereafter that Mike and I and the children moved to Westport...

It was a beautiful ranch house: the usual open kitchen/dining room, living room, and three bedrooms. There was even a garage, with a nice back yard. It was simple, and a short time later we added a little porch outside the dining room with sliding glass doors. It was a new start. I was pregnant and I hoped for the best. In hindsight, all I can hear is one of Dr. Phil's retorts, "What were you thinking?" Becoming pregnant and buying a new house wasn't the way to heal and strengthen a marriage, but again there really wasn't anyone I felt close enough to from whom to seek help or advise.

We registered at the local Catholic Church where I became the organist and choir director. One of the most telling things about my faith happened when I actually didn't have to play the organ one particular weekend. What happened? I didn't go to church! I realized that perhaps my only reason for going was because I had a job. When the job wasn't necessary, my faith came into question. The "pull" to make sure that worship was a weekly event didn't happen for many years... but that would come later.

Jason was born shortly after the move and I remember the joy in watching all three of my children together. I was a "stay-at-home" mom and it was wonderful. Those times with children go by so quickly. It's a time when life is simple and a parent has the greatest opportunity to love and teach.

We made new friends in the neighborhood and life went on in the same uncomfortable way it had when we lived in Tiverton. We were so young and didn't have any idea what a marriage and a relationship should be. Because of Mike's past indiscretion, my trust factor wasn't very high. If he didn't come home when he was supposed to, I wondered if he was with another woman, and the fact that he worked away from home a lot didn't help our relationship.

One day my worst fear happened and all my doubts were confirmed. It was Jason's third birthday and Mike was out of town. I made a phone call to the "rooming house" where he told me he was staying. Turns out that it was the home of another woman. I figured it out when I heard the sound of a child in the background. I confronted him with my suspicions and he confessed. Some time later, he came home from work and told me that he was leaving, moving to New Hampshire with this woman and her son.

What followed is pretty much a blur. There was the day he told the kids... "I'm not leaving *you;* I'm leaving your mother." I remember Jason's cry when Mike shut the door on his way out. I'll never forget the sound of his little voice: "I want my daddy!!!" It was a sound of desperation and pain—it's called weeping—that I'd never heard before...wait...I *had* heard it once before: from my father the day my mother died... As quickly as Jason's heartbreaking outburst began, it was over. Little did I know how affected he would be as he grew up.

It was clear that I was going to need to find a job. How was this going to work? Only two of my children were in school and Jason was only four years old. I learned quickly that a part- time job wouldn't work. It would cost everything I made to pay for day care. So I looked into Raytheon, even though I didn't want a full time job; it was my only choice.

Even though the day care seemed to be a great place with a bunch of happy little kids, it still killed me to drop off my little boy for a whole day. It wasn't part of my plan. I wanted to be *home* with him. I had that time with Lisa and Chris. I wanted the same with Jason. But it wasn't to be.

As near as I can remember the timeframe was late spring of 1977. Jason didn't go to daycare until September of that year. Believe it or not, Lisa took care of Christopher and Jason that summer when I went back to work. When I think about it now, DCF would probably have taken the kids away from me! Leaving a ten-year old to care for her brothers who were nine and four? What was I thinking?? Truth be known, I thought Lisa was mature enough to handle it and she never balked about it. Perhaps it helped her grow up; perhaps it took some of *her* childhood away. I've even wondered if that summer had to do with her "going off the rails" when she started college, left college, and became pregnant...all within five months. Well, that's another question that will remain forever unanswered. We do what we do at the time because it seems to be the right thing, and sometimes, it just isn't.

> *The Lord longs to be gracious to you;*
> *therefore, he will rise up*
> *to show you compassion.*
> *For the Lord is a God of justice.*
> *Blessed are all who wait for him!*
> Isaiah 30:18

That summer was a rough one for me. My Catholic upbringing taught me that a divorce is a sin, and remarriage is perhaps a worse sin. Well, of course, divorce is a sin, but it took some time before I realized that it *was* forgiveable…

There is one incident that happened during that difficult summer. It was crazy, stupid and only God could have protected me from a terrible outcome…and He did. A few friends and I had gone to a karaoke bar. It was fun. I don't drink, but we had a few laughs at what passes as "talent," and I decided to try it myself. "Hopelessly devoted to you" was my song choice. The band did a terrible job with the music and my song choice was a little too somber for the crowd to get into it. I remember thinking of the words, that my marriage had fallen apart, that love wasn't real anymore…you can just imagine my mindset. Well, I guess I wasn't all that bad because I won second place: $10!

Over that summer I went to that bar several times, mostly alone. Once again, Lisa was my sitter. She thought I had gone to the mall! Or maybe she knew that wasn't true. I've thought about that summer so many times…no cell phones…no way to get in touch with me if she needed to. My only consolation is that it was a different time, and God was watching over them as well.

The last time I went put it all into perspective. I was sitting at the bar, with my "virgin" rum and coke. A guy walked up to me and sat down. We talked. He said he remembered the night I sang and he thought I was good. A compliment always works. I don't remember what we talked about. I just remember how the conversation ended. "Your place or mine," said the guy. Naïve as I was I never saw it coming. I told him that I wasn't into what he was suggesting. The next thing he did was incredibly sad. He stood up to get a better look at himself in the mirror behind the bottles. He moved his head from side to side as if to examine every part of his face, and he said, "Why not? I'm not a bad looking guy!" How insecure can one be! Perhaps about as insecure as I was, needing to go to a bar, hoping that someone…*anyone*…would make me feel as if I had a purpose in life. I realized all that as I left the bar stool and walked to my car. The guy did follow me. We exchanged a few words, and I drove away. It was about a half hour ride, and I remember crying all the way home. What in the hell was I doing? I had three beautiful children at home; *that* was my purpose right now. Where would they be if something happened to me?

Not too long after, I met Christian Wissler Myers. He was different than anyone I had ever met before. He was a gentleman. He treated me like a lady. He was an only child. His mother was from North Carolina with a college degree. His father was a retired Navy captain, who had come up through the ranks the hard way: from the bottom. This was quite a different world for me. Highly educated people...how would I measure up? Well, it wasn't too long before I realized that at least one of them thought I was worth considering.

Raytheon had a Red Sox night at Fenway Park. A block of tickets was purchased and on sale for interested parties. Christian didn't like baseball, but he knew I did. He bought two tickets and asked me to go. Right field seats, half way between first base and the outfield, about twenty seats back. It was such fun and I just remember it was nice to have someone beside me who wanted to be with me. Little did I know that this was yet another beginning...

CHAPTER 3

23 Debra Drive
Portsmouth, Rhode Island

> Downsizing, for sure! A double-wide mobile home, creaky steps leading to the front door. Filled the bill, at the time.

In the fall of 1978 I sold the house in Westport and bought a mobile home in a park next to Raytheon off West Main Road. Selling the house was necessary because I couldn't afford it on my own and, even if I could afford it, I couldn't take care of it. So it just made sense and the mobile home was close to work. I vividly remember the yard sale on Beechwood Drive. Watching strangers handling your things and offering you much less than they're worth was both annoying and sad. It wasn't like I needed the money; I just wouldn't have the room in a mobile home. This move would need a lot of down-sizing.

It's funny how I remember little of the few days of moving into that mobile home. It could be because it was painful; it could be because it was 40 years ago! Anyway, what I do remember is the final packing which consisted of about a half-dozen green trash bags with excess items shoved in and thrown in the back of someone's truck. Those bags, interestingly enough, ended up getting thrown away nine months later when we moved again! I had never opened them the entire time we lived on Debra Drive; I figured the contents must not have been very important. So out to the trash they went. But I'm getting ahead of myself...

There are precious few memories of that time in my life, but there are a few. I remember registering Lisa and Chris for school. I made a point of informing the teachers of the pending divorce. Sometimes in cases of divorce, children act out, so I wanted to get ahead of the possibility of any behavioral problems. In those days, Lisa and Chris were two of only a couple of kids coming from divorced parents. By the time they graduated, however, kids living with their nuclear family was in the minority.

Another memory I have of that time was registering the family at St. Lucy's Catholic Church in Middletown. We went one Saturday evening—the four of us. It was very strange, first of all, because I was sitting in a pew with my children, when I was used to sitting on an organ bench with the kids close by. Perhaps the most important reason for feeling strange is because of the teachings of the church. Divorce is forbidden, and even though it hadn't happened yet, I felt as if everyone around me knew. I know that's crazy, but that's how I felt. And of course, receiving communion would definitely be out because I would be excommunicated. I actually don't remember if I went to the altar rail in defiance of the rule, or if didn't go at all. My only memory is meeting the priest in the sacristy after the service. I told him that we would like to register as parishioners. Then came the dreaded question: "Where's daddy?" he said. *How do I get out of this one*, I thought. "Daddy is working out of town," I said. Not a lie; just not the whole truth. His answer has stuck with me all these years. "Poor daddy," he said. It took me years to get over my anger. Poor daddy, indeed! There was no thought as to how difficult it might be to have three children with no present father, even in a good marriage. But that was the way it was in those days. I remember the kids looking up at me when I didn't tell the whole truth about where daddy was. I remember Christopher especially. I sometimes think he knew how hurt I was by such a comment from the priest, but that he had no knowledge of how to express himself. We left the sacristy without even giving the priest our names...and he never asked. I think I knew that this wasn't the right place for us.

One night, I arrived home from work at the usual time. My three children were at home. The mobile home park was conveniently around the corner from Raytheon, so it took only a few minutes to get home. I noticed a car that I didn't recognize next to the house. When I opened the door into the living room, there was Mike on the floor playing with 5-year old Jason and there was a woman in my kitchen, making hamburgers out of the meat I had left out to thaw that morning! This was one of those times when I wished I knew how to be a crazy woman with a frying pan who ran around whacking people she was angry with. But, that wasn't me. I simply stood there with my mouth open. She looked back at me from my kitchen as if what she was doing was perfectly normal. She even said something like she saw the thawed meat and thought she would help me! (Perhaps it was a *good* thing I wasn't

35

a crazy person!) We hadn't seen or heard from Mike in about six months. Christian was with me that night when I walked through the door, and I've often wondered why he never said or did anything. In his defense, though, the entire scene was terribly uncomfortable.

We had a few words, and after they left, the only thing I could do to express my anger was throw all the made hamburgers back into the bowl, squish them together, and remake them! I wonder if the kids ever noticed. Sounds pretty crazy, but I had to do it. *I don't need her to make dinner for my children*, I thought. Certainly a strange reaction, but at least it wasn't destructive.

Some time after that incident, the subject of church came up. Christian was an Episcopalian, which meant nothing to me. All I ever knew was "Catholic." I remember the mindset when I was growing up: *There's Catholic, and...the others, and it doesn't really matter who the "others" are because they're not going to heaven anyway.* Nobody ever said that, but everything pointed in that direction. Just like God being more of an angry God than a loving Father. I remember as a kid thinking that my father wasn't going to heaven because he was a Methodist, and I used to have a recurring dream that I was running after him, trying to baptize him! (I didn't know that Methodists were baptized Christians too). Thankfully, today I'm what they call a recovering Catholic!

Anyway, in a conversation about churches, Christian had offered to take us to Trinity Episcopal Church in Newport. I mentioned it to Lisa and Christopher, that I would take them to St. Lucy's on Saturday night and the next morning I would go to Trinity and they could come if they wanted to. Christopher didn't miss a beat. He said, "We'll go with *you*, Mom. I'm not going to that other church if they don't want you!" or something close to that. I must have discussed the church's stance on divorce with them; otherwise, how could my son have made such an amazing comment.

They didn't return to St. Lucy's. We *did* go to Trinity Church. And that was the beginning of one of the most important spiritual decisions I've made in my entire life.

Christian and I were engaged in early 1979, even before my divorce was final, and Trinity, Newport, became our church home.

36

On May 13, 1979, we were all received into the Episcopal Church. It was also Mother's Day and Christian's birthday. It was quite a day of celebration. That spring we all became very involved in the church. I joined the choir and so did the kids. We were married on July 14, 1979 and two other children became part of my life: Christian III, age 15 and Meredith, age 10. It was an interesting group when we were all together, and the family of siblings became a family in themselves. To this day, they are very close...perhaps the greatest blessing that came from my marriage to Christian...

CHAPTER 4

99 Cliff Avenue
Portsmouth, Rhode Island

> A summer home made into a year-round home. Built on a rock (no reference to Holy Scripture)...*literally* built on a rock. High up from the street, three small bedrooms, combination living/dining room, fireplace large screened-in porch. Beautiful landscaping, breathtaking sunsets...

This part of my life moved very quickly. Christian and I were seeing each other for a couple of months before I even saw the divorce lawyer. He was different from Mike in so many ways. While I had pretty much manipulated a marriage with Mike, that was so wrong. But had I not been a silly girl and Mike not very strong, I wouldn't have my three beautiful children. But I digress...

I don't remember many details of Christian's and my engagement, or the few months before that, but two things in particular do come to mind. Sometime during our short pre-engagement period, he traded in his beautiful maroon Ford Elite for a Ford station wagon! Out of the blue—with no warning. I recall Meredith commenting on the day he drove the wagon into the driveway at his mother's house, while Meredith and Christian were looking out the second floor window, wondering what their father had done with his beautiful car! Obviously he was thinking of the necessity of more room in his vehicle for four or five children.

The second thing I remember was my one appointment with the divorce lawyer. The meeting looked like a scene from a Law and Order episode. He was tall, quite good-looking, wearing pressed trousers with suspenders, and a snow white, long sleeve shirt with perfect creases from shoulder to wrist. He had asked me if I was seeing anyone and if it was serious. I hedged the issue. He came around the desk, leaned on the wall beside me, folded his arms in front of him, put one foot up on a corner chair, and said, "If you're seeing someone and getting serious this soon, you'll be back in this office again before you know it!" I never forgot that. Little did I know...

I've always been very particular about where I lived; yet, I don't really recall how the Cliff Avenue house became an option, except for the fact that it was Christian's parents "vacation" home. Vacation home? But they lived in Newport, and there was a "summer home" twenty miles north? I didn't have to understand it. It just was! And how it all happened that it became ours is a mystery to me. In hindsight, it makes me think of how Mike and I came to own the house on Hooper St. It seemed to have... just happened; one day we were renting it from my father, and the next we were sitting in the bank, signing papers. Cliff Avenue happened even simpler than that. Unless I've totally forgotten, I don't remember anything about a bank appointment. We became the owners of his parent's vacation home....or maybe Chris became the owner. Who knows?!

It was originally built as a summer home in an area called The Hummocks. Several of the neighbors who came to The Hummocks in the summer to get out of the city were from the same family in the Boston area. All of the homes in the area were fairly small, and so was this one. It had three small bedrooms with walls that didn't go all the way up to the ceiling. That was to allow air to flow which helped during the hot summer months. As I think about it now, it was definitely too small for five people, and later six when Meredith came to live with us during the week. But somehow we made it work. The kid's bedrooms were the same with bunk beds and a closet on one side and a desk with two chairs on the other, and there were drawers under the bottom bunks. By today's standards, these kids were amazing, living in such close quarters. I never heard any complaints from anyone. Thinking about it now, it's almost unbelievable.

Christian's grandmother had died three months before we were married and we acquired her dining room set and hutch. Almost twenty years of dinners, holiday celebrations, birthdays, babies, and everything you can think of happened around that table. This very table will come up again under the Florida address in a very strange way, a way that changed me drastically.

Christian and I were married in 1979 on July 14th. What do I remember about that day? Just a couple of things. My first memory happened in the bedroom on Cliff Avenue an hour or so before the wedding. Christian, Christopher and Jason had spent the night in Newport. Lisa and Meredith stayed with me. While I

July 13, 1979
Trinity Church, Newport, RI

was combing Lisa's hair before we left for the church, I flashed back to my first wedding. I thought of how different it was. The first time I had a beautiful white dress, my parents were there, and of course a photographer! There was a limo waiting to take me and my attendants to the church.

When I came back to reality, I was standing in my bedroom in a lovely blue dress, helping my daughter with her hair and I was about to drive myself to the church! My mother had died when I was 21, and my father was at home in Tiverton, recuperating from a hospital stay dealing with COPD. It was a fleeting moment of many different thoughts, but I did say to myself, "What am I doing?" I was sure it was simply wedding jitters, so I dismissed it.

The second thought I have about that day happened after the wedding, standing outside the church. We'd had a small reception in Honeyman Hall with a few people in attendance. We were getting ready to leave for the Poconos, and I told Christian that I wanted to go see my father. He had been unable to come to the wedding because it was a very hot, humid day and his breathing issues meant he had to stay home close to a fan. I wasn't that close to my father but for some reason I wanted him to see me in that beautiful blue dress. Closeness be damned, I think every little girl wants to make her father smile on her wedding day, or maybe I just wanted his blessing. Well, Christian's response to my request was that we couldn't go because it would get us to our first stop in Connecticut at least an hour later than he had planned. I didn't argue...I *should* have. The rest of our marriage might have been different in many ways if I had pressed the issue. But I didn't. I didn't see my father that day, and we left for Pennsylvania. That was 1979.

My father died a year later and I have little else to say about that. I do remember visiting him in the hospital right after he had tried to slit his wrists...with a safety razor. Why? We never knew. Perhaps he was tired of being sick, or lonely, and didn't know how to handle life any more. We were never a family who said "I love you" in conversation, so what he said that day was memorable and sad.

Ella, Buddy, Maureen and me
1979

When I stood next to his bed and looked at the bandages on his wrists, he looked at me and said, "I don't know why I did that; I love you," to which I said, "We love you too, dad." How sad that "we" was all I could say; "I" wasn't on my radar! Is it any wonder that for so many years of my life I failed at love? One has to be transparent and totally open where love is concerned or it doesn't work. It took me many more years to figure that out...

One special spiritual awakening for me happened at a church in Darien, Connecticut. It was the early 80s and there was a Holy Spirit awakening happening all over the Northeast. I had learned about Terri Fullam, an Episcopal priest who was setting the state on fire. He had a little church that had outgrown its seating *and* standing capacity. They had moved their Sunday services to a local high school auditorium. Chris and I attended one Sunday and it was unforgettable.

On the left side of the stage was a baby grand piano and on the right side was the altar. The auditorium was packed like sardines. People had their hands in the air even before the music began. I was pretty new to the gifts of the Spirit and I'm sure that Chris was uncomfortable, but he didn't say anything. We found two seats down in the front and waited for the service to begin. It was 9am. Then Terri appeared, complete with chasuble and charisma, and it was clear this was going to be a one-man event. He played the piano magnificently. He taught the thousand people a new

41

song. He preached. He celebrated. He sang. I was in heaven! And each part of the service was building to what would happen at communion.

While over one thousand people came forward for communion, a woman in front of me turned around and asked me if I had something I wanted to pray for. I was taken aback. Before I knew it she had me in front of the seats, along with dozens of other people being prayed for. There were people slain in the Spirit. There were others speaking in tongues. Still others were in ecstasy, arms raised in prayer. Strangely, I was calm. I wasn't used to this, but on that day, it seemed alright. She smiled at me and said, "What would you like to pray for, dear?" I didn't miss a beat. I said, "I would like my husband to have the same feelings about all this that I do." We prayed, nothing spectacular happened, and I went back to my seat. The service ended three house later! We drove back to Rhode Island and I don't recall us ever talking about the event. I guess I was afraid of what he might say. Maybe I was afraid the prayer wouldn't work. I never knew if it did or not. But for me? That was surely one of the first events that would lead me to where I was meant to be.

> *Do not fear, for I have redeemed you;*
> *I have called you by name,*
>
> *you are mine.*
> Isaiah 43:1

In January 1981, a fire ignited in my spiritual journey that has never gone out. Both Christian and I attended a Cursillo. Cursillo is a Spanish word that means "little course." It's a Thursday evening to Sunday afternoon Christian event, jam-packed with 15 talks on various life subjects, singing, worship, food, and special notes from just about everybody we knew. It was an eye-opening time for me. That was the weekend that I discovered that God really loved me. I had grown up thinking that God and my father were around every corner, waiting for me to do something wrong. God *wasn't* waiting for me to do something wrong; he *loved* me! What an amazing discovery!

The weekend led me into a deeper relationship with God. While you can attend only one Cursillo as a candidate, a person can be on the team of folks who make the weekend happen. I was on at least five of six teams over the next couple of years. The Holy Spirit revival sensation was so vibrant that there was a Cursillo every other month for many years with at least fifty candidates on each weekend! It was incredible. Each Cursillo deepened my desire to grow closer and closer to God. Little did I know where it would lead. I became a Eucharistic Minister and my church involvement became more personal.

Life was busy, full and sometimes complicated, but for the most part, it was good. The blended family grew together and there was never talk about "step" children or "step" brothers and sisters. We were a family. In fact, Christian ended up adopting Lisa, Christopher and Jason.

As the years went on, there were typical children issues that we dealt with, but we survived. What do I remember? Band concerts, hockey games, parades, proms, etc. Personally, I dealt with too many self-esteem issues to list them all. But I managed to work through them and get up the next day to face whatever was to come. Amidst those issues, God had a plan that I would have never expected. Following the 1981 Cursillo, both Christian and I became involved with the Rhode Island Cursillo movement by becoming team members on other weekends. The diocese held six weekends a year around that time and it took quite a few people to put on a weekend. We were both chosen as team members for six or seven weekends and in January 1984, I ended up being the rector (the lay leader) of the weekend. And so it began...

For some time before that 1984 weekend, I had been sensing what the church has named "a call" to the priesthood. I didn't recognize it as such. It was just a feeling...a nudging at my heart, if you will...but whatever it was I dismissed it. It had only been about six years since women were allowed to be ordained. I didn't know any women priests, and the whole thing seemed utterly ridiculous. I had been out of school for twenty years. I had no college education. I had four children at home, a full time job, and...well, you get the point. This idea wasn't a good one, and I kept it all to myself.

Then came the Cursillo weekend of January 1984. It was Sunday morning shortly after midnight. I had been troubled with thoughts about this "call." Spending three solid days steeped in spiritual readings and teachings kept the issue in the forefront and I was having difficulty setting it aside. I walked in to the chapel.

It was quiet...dark except for the sanctuary lamp near the tabernacle. I don't know what came over me, but I walked to the front of the altar, got down on my knees and eventually found myself flat on the floor, face down, and I cried, "What do you want??" Clear as a bell, as if a man was standing beside me, I heard the words, "Go to school." Well, Mary, Joan of Arc, St. Teresa...they all heard voices, but if I recollect, the voices said things that made sense! What on earth did *go to school* mean? After I got over the shock, I got up from the floor and walked toward my room. On the way I decided to knock on the door of my friend who was one of the clergy on the weekend. A coincidence? Not a chance!

At that time in the history of the Diocese of Rhode Island six Cursillos were being held a year with three priests on each Cursillo staff. What were the odds that Lorne Coyle, my home church rector, would have been on the very weekend where God planned to *call* me?

It was one o'clock in the morning. I knocked on his door—I needed to talk to someone or I would explode! I relayed what happened in the chapel and what I had been feeling for some time, and his answer was simple: "If God is calling you to be a priest, you need a college degree, so you *do* have to go to school!" That was *not* what a thirty-six year old wife and mother with a full time job and four children at home wanted to hear. But it was a fact.

After the weekend was over I remember thinking...now what? I was afraid to tell anyone for fear they would think I was crazy, or worse yet, laugh at the thought of me becoming a priest. Actually, *I* even thought it was funny. But I learned very quickly that God will lead if you let him, and if he wants something to happen, it will.

Discernment is a very important part of coming to know the will of God. I might want to take a particular path in life, but unless others can see that the path in me as well, there's a good chance

44

that I could be seeking my own will instead of God's. So, over the next couple of months, I sent a dozen or so letters to my closest friends on that Cursillo weekend, telling them what had happened to me and what I thought God was saying to me. And I asked their opinion, their discernment. As I think about it now, I was looking for their approval, not realizing that the discernment of others is a critical factor in someone's call to the ministry. It turned out that I received a resounding "yes" and "go for it" from everyone I had contacted! Now, I had to tell Christian.

I remember he was standing at the stove, stirring something, and I told him the whole story. He said five strange words: "What took you so long?" Perhaps he sensed what was going on within me. Maybe God had spoken to him as well...he never said. Now the issue was, what do I do next?

The thought of The University of Rhode Island in Kingston—*I can't do that; I've never driven that far in my life—and what about my job? The kids? My church responsibilities?* Someone told me about Barrington College, a small Christian school in Barrington, RI, not that far away. So I looked into it. Mind you, I knew nothing about college. Nothing! I didn't even know that there was such a thing as night school until I spoke to the college counselor. After that first visit, I was amazed how smoothly everything went! I registered for one class in September 1984: New Testament Survey. It was wonderful, but it took a little time get used to getting home from work, having dinner ready (with the help of all the kids!) going to class, and getting home about 10pm. But it worked. I thought this was going to be the road God had planned for me.

But partway through the semester, the college announced that it was closing this particular campus and merging with Amherst College outside of Boston! *Really, God? You've got to be kidding! Now what?* In hindsight, I think God's plan was "baby steps." Taking this one course at a small college at least showed me that I *could* actually accomplish something like this. Now I had to look at URI, whether I liked it or not. And once again, God's plan went into action.

I made my first appointment with a counselor and, ironically—just that year—the college had opened up a new degree program at night called Bachelor of General Studies (BGS). The requirements would be the same as for a BS or a BA, but the core requirements would be "generalized"—hence the name of the degree, specifically designed for people who had been out of school for at least twenty years and wanted to earn a degree without necessarily choosing a particular major. I remember my first interview with a delightful man—his name was Cleveland—who brought out more confidence in me than I ever thought I had. I began to think that God might actually know what he was doing with my life!

The next eight years were jam-packed: a full time job, a husband and four children at home, two courses a semester, one course in the summer, a strict schedule two nights a week with dinner and school, the usual family issues, school events and an occasional problem or two. When I think back on those years, I am truly amazed that it all happened as smoothly as it did. Oh, don't get me wrong; there was some family drama. If one has a family, there will *always* be drama. But for such a long hall, my children were amazing with all their help; however, I'm smart enough to know that things probably went on that shouldn't have. But God watched out for them as well. I've often wondered if they ever felt short changed or if they were proud of what I was trying to do. Years later, though, I learned how they felt, and it was good…

In those days college was a lot cheaper than it is today, and I was able to pay for it by saving a small portion of my salary on a weekly basis. I was seven years into my college career, with one year left to go, when the bottom fell out.

There was a restructuring at Raytheon Company where I worked. A certain number of employees who had been there the shortest length of time were laid off, along with one secretary from every department. Even though I had been there for 13 years, I was the "low man on the totem pole" in my section. If I was laid off, there would be no saved money to finish my degree. How was this all going to work out? I actually wondered if Chris would be willing to financially support my last year. That might sound like a strange question, but I remember thinking that all through those seven years of night school, I don't remember any conversations with him, supportive or otherwise. We just did what we did. *That's the saddest sentence I've written so far...we just did what we did.* We both worked and came home. We had dinner together, all six of us. Two nights a week, I went to school. We had a "date night" on Fridays. If I try really hard, I can remember a few of those Friday nights, mostly about our favorite restaurant—The Chart House—*not* about the company or the conversation. As I look back all these years later, I think how sad that was. We talked about the kids but there wasn't much in the way of personal conversation. Again, in hindsight, Chris didn't know how to be vulnerable to another human being, even one he was supposed to love...

In the winter semester of 1986, Lisa went through a very difficult time in her life. It was a time when all the love and attention in the world couldn't fix the problem and I was filled with lots of emotions. Those emotions got in the way of my school work and I was sure that I would fail that semester. I entertained thoughts of quitting school because I felt I couldn't be a mother and survive school too. My courses that semester? Greek Mythology and Ancient Philosophy! Enough said! Courses like that would make *anyone* want to quit! I was drowning in feelings of failure both in school and as a mother, and Christian said one simple thing to me when I mentioned quitting school. He said: "This too shall pass." It did, but not without a lot of heartache along with life-changing experiences for Lisa.

Back to being laid off from Raytheon. When my rector Lorne Coyle learned that I might have financial difficulties with my last year of school, he dipped into a church scholarship fund and provided for my last year's tuition! At the same time, I took a part time secretarial job at the local Baptist Church in Middletown. One might say that things were smoothing out and I could see the finish line ahead. But wait...another setback was on the horizon. While I was working on my senior project, I had a minor car accident. I remember it well. I was driving back to Portsmouth from Newport after a meeting with my spiritual director; it was Maundy Thursday afternoon. Just as I approached a green traffic light in the travel lane, the car to my left stopped and motioned to an oncoming car to cross traffic in front of me. It was a bad idea!

I was hit in the front quarter of my car, bringing me to a stop just as I was about to hit a street sign pole. Have you ever been in a car accident? It's a very unusual experience. The entire thing happens in second, but it feels like minutes as you seem to experience it in slow motion. It's very strange indeed. An ambulance arrived along with the police. The responders attended to the driver of the other car as well as myself. I was a little dazed and tried to get out of the car, but a nice young man told me to be still for a minute. Then he asked me a question: "Did you bang your face on the steering wheel?" to which I responded, "No, I've always looked like this." *Where did that come from?* Strange things can come out your mouth when you are under duress. Poor man, the way he looked at me after I said that! I wondered what he thought. Then when they said they were going to tow my car, I said, "Where? I have library books in the back seat!" Another bizzare comment! Oh, well, what can I say. There are no instructions how to act when one is in an accident situation.

When they put me in the rescue truck, I looked over at the young man who had hit my car. I asked him if he was all right and all he said was, "My dad is going to kill me!" A typical teenage comment; surely he was driving dad's car! I looked at my watch and, realizing that it was 2:30pm, I figured the young man was just coming home from school. I asked him where he went to school, and he said 'Portsmouth High.' "Oh," I said, "Do you know my son Jason." Wrong thing to say! The poor kid just about had a stroke. "Oh, my God. I hit my friend's mother!" Actually it was kind of funny, and neither of us was very hurt, although I did end up with a broken knuckle that kept me in the hospital over night for surgery the next morning to insert a pin. Now, with my left hand out of commission, I needed help typing my senior project. I supplied the information and another secretary at Raytheon put it together while I was having physical therapy on my left hand. Nothing is easy…

May 1991 – URI Graduation. It was a little non-descript for me, perhaps because I was part of the smaller night school group that was incorporated into the thousands of young people from the day college. The more I've tried to remember that day, the less I can recall. A few pictures that we took come to mind…a vague memory of a dinner with some classmates, my hair being very blonde because I had sprayed it with some concoction that, combined with the sun, lightens your hair. Strange memories. Perhaps it was because that graduation wasn't so important to me; it was just another event, another milestone to check off before I got to where I was intending to go. The prize was still quite a-ways away...

Over the next few months there must have been at least one meeting with my rector and the bishop and at least one or two meetings with the COM (Commission on Ministry). This is the diocesan committee whose sole purpose is to screen persons who feel they have a call to the ordained ministry. Back in those days I did a lot of journaling, and it is from those notes that the next chapters begin.

(This is probably a good place to interject the over-arching issue that followed me around throughout my entire ordination process: I was a conservative female, and I was totally unaware that this would be an issue. In some dioceses, being a female would have been enough to stop the ordination process, but in RI, a *conservative* female wasn't going to make it. I say this up front because just about everything that happened from this time until I was dropped from the ordination process a week before seminary graduation had to do with being a conservative female, although it was never spoken.)

In January 1992 I started my year of discerning at St. Peter's Church in Narragansett. Anyone who feels a call to the ministry is assigned to a parish for one year where a committee of a few meet monthly with the postulant (that's what a person seeking to be ordained is called in the beginning). The postulant gets to "play priest," if you will. Although unable to bless or consecrate, I could do just about everything else, and from the start it felt perfectly natural: serving the chalice, reading the lessons, setting the table—all of it came very easily to me. It was as if I'd been doing it forever. One of the first things I did in the parish was to send out invitation letters to 27 kids and teens asking them to become acolytes and torch bearers.

Now it was time to start looking into seminaries, which one would work for me. Chris and I had visited TESM (Trinity School for Ministry) in Ambridge, PA, a short time after my car accident. It was a fairly new seminary but it was definitely "on the map" as far as the conservative branch of the Church was concerned and I knew that I might have trouble getting the bishop to allow me to enroll there. Knowing what I wanted was going to be an uphill battle, I struggled between worry and trust. One side of me knew that righteousness would prevail, that tradition and God's will would triumph, but the other side of me was frightened that I'd get sucked up in the crazy contemporary issues and become cynical, losing track of what the ministry really is. I prayed that my foundation would be enough to get me through.

A combination of the intern meetings and a Lenten retreat had me looking at my "scars," negative memories of the past, insecurities of who I was and what I hoped I could become. One committee member had made the remark that the past couldn't have been *that* bad, considering where I was at that point. That's when I started thinking of how everything we experience is part of the formation process, how the past helps form the future. It's not always easy to experience certain things, but when we look at them in the light of what we are becoming, change becomes easier...or at least tolerable!

> *Where there is strife, there is pride,*
> *but wisdom is found in those*
> *who take advice.*
> Proverbs 13:10

Somewhere in this time period, I attended a retreat, and it surely gave me much to think about. In particular, the retreat was centered around *The Jesus Prayer*, a prayer that is still with me to this day:

> *Lord Jesus Christ, Son of God,*
> *have mercy on me, a sinner.*

This prayer is sometimes used in mediation exercises with the four phrases connected to breathing out...and breathing in. Well, my first introduction to the prayer wasn't positive; it sounded like I was unworthy of the Lord's time, let alone his forgiveness. But after the way the retreat leader approached the prayer, everything changed. Now, all of a sudden, this Jesus *was* mercy and it was being showered upon me, for no other reason other than I was loved by *this God*. What a concept...perhaps the beginning of me *really* understanding the God I wanted so much to serve as a priest. I left that retreat clinging to one phrase from Philippians: "I can do all things in Him who strengthens me." I put that uplifting passage on a 3 x 5 card and taped it to my bathroom mirror. That passage would become more and more important to me as the process continued...

Another part of the process is the monthly meeting of interns with the diocesan representative. While these meetings are supposed to be among "peers," it became extremely clear that it was not like that at all. Some in the group had already graduated from seminary; some were transfers from other dioceses. My old fears began to bubble up. And right about this time, my brother, who was in Florida, had a brain aneurysm. It didn't take long before all my old fears and insecurities surfaced again...that's because when there is a family crisis, old insecurities bubble up. So here I was, trying to find my place in the future and dealing with issues of the past...yet again. I was very fragile, and when my brother died a week later, it seemed as if there was little future. With so many years between us, I didn't really know him and it was hard to watch my sisters mourning a brother that in principle wasn't mine to mourn. I remember others in the family questioning my lack of reaction to my brother's death, that I didn't care. No one could know what I was feeling since I was having my own problems understanding it myself. The first real breakdown was when I told my sister that my grief wasn't like theirs, that my grief was burying just another relative that I didn't know! That's when I wept, harder than I think I ever had in my life. *Why then*, I wondered. Maybe it was because of a feeling of loss...something that never was and never would be...just like my mother. This was one of those times when God used extreme pain to bring me a hint of joy. When I had told my sister that I always felt disconnected from my brother, she told me how he used to lie on the floor and play with me when I was a baby; he was 19 years old when I was born. Shortly thereafter he went into the service, and one time when my sister had written him a letter, she had casually mentioned that "mother got a prescription for Elizabeth and she's better." His response was to call home, all upset, wanting to know what was wrong with the baby! A nice memory...a hint of love, of the presence of God in a dysfunctional family. Nevertheless, it was another strange building block in the story of one destined for something completely different.

CHAPTER 5
Virginia Theological Seminary
Alexandria, Virginia

> From a house to a dorm...*ONE ROOM*...with a bed, a chair and a desk!

I had done an extensive comparative study of all the Episcopal Seminaries in the country. There was one in Boston, but that wouldn't work for me. It was very liberal. Then there was TESM that we had visited, but the Bishop wasn't supportive of that one because it was still fairly new and its slant conservative. So I took it upon myself to look into the others in a comparative way, and VTS, Virginia Theological Seminary, seemed to be the right choice, mostly because of its location. Chris often had meetings in Washington, and when he had such a meeting, we could spend a weekend together. We had friends who lived in Alexandria, actually across the street from the seminary. That's where we could stay on his visits. It seemed like the best option. The seminary dean wasn't so sure.

I remember a meeting we had months before I made the choice to attend VTS. She was a little surprised to learn that we wouldn't be coming together. She said that seminary was a major event in the life of a married couple and that it was important that each person "grow together" in this experience. We assured her that we had been married for 15 years and that we would be fine. Little did we know...

Sometime in August 1994 we packed up the Taurus station wagon and off we drove to Alexandria, Virginia, to what would be the most powerful change in my life ever.

It was a whirlwind, moving furniture up to the second floor of Wilmer Hall. My dorm room was right at the top of the stairs, overlooking the grounds of the seminary. There were three dorms at the seminary: a men's dorm, a woman's dorm, and my dorm. Wilmer Hall was coed. Now that might sound strange, but almost all of us were *older* than the usual age, coming right out of college. We were sort of an odd group, from all over the country...actually the world! Yet, we grew together over those three years.

As I think about the day Chris left and I was alone—actually for the *first time in my adult life*—no spouse, no kids—it was incredibly frightening and lonely. Chris took the Alexandria train back to DC where he would catch a flight home. But what I remember most is our "goodbye." It was very strange. It was devoid of anything that resembled a married couple who were about to be separated for God knows how long. Certainly it was nothing like you see in the movies. And that shouldn't have surprised me. Chris was never overly demonstrative with his feelings; but I guess I expected more. As the train pulled away, reality came quickly. There I was...in the middle of a train station, walking back to the car to drive the few blocks back to the seminary...alone! Could I do this? Too late to ask that; it was a done deal!

My new dorm family

Back at the seminary, the incoming class of juniors would be alone on campus for two weeks before the rest of the students would arrive. (To clarify, a first year seminary student is called a junior. A second year student is called a middler, and a third year student is a senior). Juniors spent the first two weeks on campus dealing with a lot of orientation and a couple of programs that applied only to juniors.

I remember the awkwardness of meeting new people—that has never been easy for me; I'm insecure by nature. So, all in all, this experience was close to traumatic for me! After dinner in the refectory, I went back to my room, sat down on my bed and just cried! Now it was all sinking in! *Whatever made me think I could do this? I'm almost old enough to be the mother of some of these kids! I don't have very good reading or study habits. And I left my daughter pregnant with my first grandchild! What was I thinking?*

Over the next few days I began to realize that for the first time in my life I had to take care of myself, that no one was depending on me for anything. I was truly on my own. Boy, did I have a lot of time on my hands! At least for a *short* time anyway!

For the next three years, seminary was an amazing experience. I found myself doing things I never thought I could do, being involved in things that were so foreign to me, but I managed. I remember my first class: 9am—Monday, Wednesday, Friday—Old Testament. It was in a lecture hall—multiple rows, tiered from top to bottom—seating for maybe one hundred, at long tables left to right. I'd never seen anything like that before. My college experience was *so* much smaller. My anxiety went from bad to worse when Dr. Newman handed out his syllabus. *What's a syllabus*, I thought? It was becoming quite clear that my type of college experience had not prepared me for this! I think there were about thirty books on the list, with the expectation that we would peruse, if not read, every one of them …and this course was only one semester! I was overwhelmed before I took my first test…

Twenty-three years have gone by since that first day and that particular course turned out to be a turning point, but I didn't know it at the time. The seminary had a policy that I was unaware of: if a student received two failing grades in consecutive semesters, they would be asked to leave the seminary! In my first semester, I received a D in Greek; in my second semester I received a D in Old Testament. Needless to say I was upset, but God managed to use this situation yet again. A student that I was close to had a suggestion: "Why don't you ask Dr. Newman to give you extra credit work to bring up your grade?" *You can do that?* I said. I was so far out of my league I was beginning to wonder whom I was kidding, thinking that for one minute I would become a priest. And to go and talk to a professor? You've got to be kidding! It wasn't until I received the revised grade of "C"—after I had done the extra work—that I learned about the "two Ds policy." I began to think that something bigger than me was at work here. *Maybe I was really called to be a priest…* Time would tell.

I fell in love with the routine of seminary: 8am, chapel; classes beginning at 9:15am; lunch at 12; classes at 1pm; back to the dorm usually by 4pm; dinner at 6pm. I remember the walk from the

54

dorm, up the little hill to that beautiful chapel with 150 years of history. It's actually gone now. There was a fire a few years after I graduated that was caused by a cleaning rag left too close to an old cast iron radiator in the sacristy. All that was left was the bell tower. What a sad day that was. They did rebuild, but while the outside matches all the other red brick seminary buildings, the inside is quite modern. I guess it serves the purpose of the day, but nothing could replace the old style with its pews, chancel and high altar.

But back to the daily routine. I guess it wasn't so much the *entire* daily routine that I loved. It was the *story* that continued every day. What do I mean by that? Well, we have the BCP, the Book of Common Prayer, we have liturgy, and we have a lectionary—a pattern to follow whereas—if the lectionary is followed—one can read just about the entire Bible in three years. And this was the part I looked forward to. With every reading, the *story* was continued. Each day in the usual three readings, we heard the greatest story every told. Day after day, the readings unfolded the amazing story of creation, the fall, our redemption, and all the crazy details in between. I couldn't wait for each chapel service to begin so I could hear the next chapter.

Another remembrance: There was a 'common room' on the ground floor of every dorm...it was like your home living room, complete with a television, and it was open to anyone at anytime. In that little room, we had birthday parties, Christmas parties, prayer meetings, just about anything you can think of that might happen in someone's living room. It was in my common room that I was first introduced to Seinfeld! And it was crazy. Every weekday night at 9pm we met in this room for Evening Prayer or Compline, but on Thursdays, it was 9:30 for prayer—*after* Seinfeld. I even found a large framed poster of Cramer, and it hung in our dorm common room for three years. I wonder what happened to that poster?

While the enormous amount of reading that I was never able to accomplish and the never-ending struggle with memorization took its toll on my self-esteem, there was a light moment one morning in my New Testament class. As a back story, the longest amount of time that Chris and I were separated while I was in seminary was about six weeks. He often traveled to Washington DC for Raytheon and he tried to plan his trips close to the weekend. We stayed at Bob and Emma Jo's house in Alexandria which was practically across the street from the seminary. On one of these "sleep-overs" Emma Jo's daughter Catherine showed us an alarm clock that she had purchased: it was a chicken wearing sun glasses, holding a guitar—I think it was supposed to be an Elvis look-a-like. The belly of the guitar was the clock, and when the alarm went off, it played guitar music and a raspy voice said, "Heeeeeey...... yeeeeah....... wake up baby, come and dance with me!" It was a riot! And I had a thought: *what a cool thing to show some other students. Maybe it might help me fit in with the younger crowd.* If you ever have a thought like that, you'd be smart to dismiss it.

I took the clock to my New Testament class. I was sitting in the third row close to the end. There was some time before Dr. Vandavelder would be there, so I took it out and showed it to a couple of people sitting around me. They thought it was really funny. And here's where my common sense dissolved and my need to 'fit in' kicked in. "Why don't you set the clock for 9:45am and put it under Dr. Vandevelder's podium?" One of the guys came up with that idea, and I saw it as an opportunity to be one of them. I'd never done *anything* like this before, but my need to 'fit in' was greater than my common sense. So I did it! When Dr. Vandevelder walked in and down to his podium, I knew I was screwed! The guys were all silently chuckling to themselves...and I was sweating bullets!

The lecture was from the Book of Isaiah. Half way into the class—about 9:45am—Dr. Vandevelder read the words: "O Lord, can these dry bones live?" And, yes—you guessed it: "Heeeeeey...... yeeeeah....... wake up baby, come and dance with me!" Those who knew what it was, laughed uncontrollably while I thought my face was going to explode! It was beet red! What I *didn't* know was, the insane music and talking wouldn't stop until it was shut off manually. Sweet Dr. Vandevelder, who was apparently accustomed to junior pranks, just stood still, his hands holding the front edges of the podium. It was as if he was frozen in that spot. He simply looked forward, perfectly still. All I could think of was: *Isn't one of the guys going to save me? Wouldn't someone go and retrieve the clock?* Fat chance! After hearing the same thing three or four times, I had to move. I ran down the stairs to the podium, and reaching under the podium, I said with a sick smile on my face, "Oh, it's just an alarm clock."

The professor looked like he'd been shot. He was old. I'm glad he didn't have a heart attack. I didn't think about his age when I lost my senses.

Later at lunch, he actually came and sat at my table and we talked about the incident. Such a sweet man. He *was* old and didn't really realize what it was all about at all. He thought it was a malfunctioning tape player, recording his lecture! His only comment was, "Well, at least it wasn't in chapel!" It's amazing the crazy things we do to fit in...

My first trip home in 1994 was the weekend of Thanksgiving, and it was somewhat traumatic. To put this into writing seems so ridiculous; I guess it just shows how insecure I was at the time. To back up a little, before I left for seminary Chris had wanted me to clear off and pack away the two big shelves that separated the living room and dining room. Why? I had no idea, and I never questioned him. It wasn't as if he was going to have to dust the books. So I did what he asked. With such a large open space, with multiple empty shelves, it really made the rooms look uninhabited. So many personal items gone, and the house felt cold and unwelcoming. Adding to this, I noticed something very different when I walked into the kitchen after almost twelve weeks: the items on the shelves in the kitchen had been rearranged. Now before you think I've become neurotic, remember: Before seminary, this was *my* home. *I* had done all the decorating, etc. I was reasonably happy here. My children grew up here. It was home. But my insecurity grew larger, and what I saw was an attempt to erase any hint of "the woman" who used to live here. Thinking about it now—so many years later—it was traumatic, but like so many other things in my life, I don't remember saying anything about it. I guess it wasn't time for me to be the person God intended me to be.

Except for a few minor setbacks, seminary was a wonderful, rewarding experience. Besides the theology and Scripture and practical application that I had come there to learn, who I was supposed to be began to emerge, little by little...much of that learning coming from my field education parish. During the first year of seminary we were tasked to attend a different church every week in search of just the 'right' one in which to spend the next two years of Sundays doing field work. And once again, this assignment wasn't without problems.

There were about 60 students in my Junior Class all of us traveling every Sunday to a different parish in the greater Alexandria/Washington area and its surrounding cities. If we found a parish we liked, it was up to us to speak to the rector and find out if he or she would be willing to take on a seminarian. Week after week went by. More and more students were settled for the coming year while a handful of us were still searching. I had interviewed at a couple of churches, but someone else had been chosen. It was getting pretty close to the end of the school year when I found a church. Not many details are still in my memory, but there are enough to share.

It was pretty little church in Alexandria, and at this point, I was running out of time. In hindsight, it was all about 'settling' with what I had found. There weren't many other choices, or at least I hadn't found any. I set up an appointment with the rector and when the meeting happened, I should have trusted my instincts.

The office was lovely…lots of period furniture and the decorating was exquisite. The rector came around his desk, greeted me with a handshake, and we sat in two antique side chairs with an elaborate accessory table between us. I remember him sitting back in his chair, sticking his chest out and looking across at the "I Love Me" wall that was behind his desk. (That name comes from a quarter class I took in my senior year…I'll get back to that later.) There was something off, but I couldn't put my finger on it. But what choice did I have? It was almost time to go home for the summer and I needed a parish assignment in place. We talked; he accepted me into the program, and he said we'd talk in September.

Some time in early July, I received a phone call from the office of the Assistant Bishop of Virginia. I was told that my assignment at the church in Virginia was cancelled and I was to meet with the Bishop when I returned to seminary in September. *Okay, God, what's going on now?* There were times I felt just when my path was becoming manageable, another pothole appeared.

In September I learned that the Rector had been removed from the parish, having been accused of sexual misconduct. It seems that during the summer a woman had gone to the bishop with

58

allegations. The Bishop had a meeting with the parish; the rector wasn't invited. During the meeting to discuss the one allegation, several other women stood up with similar allegations. Before the summer was over, the Rector was removed and the church was in a rector search. I definitely dodged a bullet there, but now I was without a parish—in fact, I was the *only* student without a parish in which to accomplish my field work!

> *Take my yoke upon you and learn from me,*
> *for I am gentle and humble in heart,*
> *and you will find rest for your souls.*
> Matthew 11:29

I don't remember how I was introduced to St. Timothy's in Herndon, Virginia, but it was a wonderful addition to my education and my introduction to life as a priest. I spent two years working under Fr. Brad Rundlett and I wish I could remember all the experiences I had because they really introduced me to real parish life. I have a notebook that was given to me the last day I was there, and it's filled with notations and best wishes from parish members. In looking at it recently, on the first page is written: "You have made a lasting impression upon me, and many other people. Thank you! I am confident of your call, and the gifts you have been given to serve our God and Savior. Go in peace to love and serve the Lord..." and it was signed, "Brad." Funny, I never thought about the impact I might have made on St. Timothy's and it warms my heart as I reflect on that time in my life.

Besides serving at two services every Sunday, I was required to take part in a parish discernment committee. The individuals on this committee were tasked to walk this two-year walk with me, to help me learn and grow in my chosen vocation. And again, this group of individuals became important to me. There were wonderful worship services, baptisms, dinners, parties, glorious Easters, and so many intimate relationships. Yet even as I write that, it's true that the things we remember most are those things that were painful or outrageous.

59

One such incident was a man who always looked lost when he came to church on Sunday. He did not show up for a few Sundays and the day he returned, I cornered him before service. I suggested we sit in the church for a bit and talk. Turns out that he had been on a suicide mission and because of a phone call from his sister who needed him, he put down the gun that he had held to his head...and he came to his senses. He also said that he needed to be here so he could talk to me because some things I had said had helped him realize that he needed to trust God, that he was worth it. How is it that other people could see a healing vessel in me when I couldn't?

So much of who I am changed during this next phase of my life. As I thought about St. Timothy's, how important they became to me, and as I read more of what people said the day I left that church, I actually began to realize the depth of the changes that happened next. I'm over two decades from these events and as I write these words I'm reminded of a song that probably speaks to the rest of my journey. The title is "Broken Things." The words tell the story of how God uses the least likely people to accomplish His work here on earth, and I think that says it all—not just for me, but for *all* of us. We're all broken and yet God uses us to do his work. As the next phase of this story speaks to brokenness and disappointment, there is redemption in the end. I had to refer to my journals because one forgets details, and some details at this stage were very important.

In January 1995 I had returned to Rhode Island for a Candidacy meeting with the COM (Commission on Ministry). By this time in the process, a postulant has become a candidate for a year; this was to be my *second* candidacy interview, and the outcome was the same as the first. I didn't dazzle the COM, but I didn't say anything heretical either. They had received my letter describing my activities since last April. In the letter I talked about CPE (Clinical Pastoral Education). This 10-week program occurs during the summer before the second year of seminary. In it one serves as a hospital chaplain two days a week, and works the other three days with a small group of peers. The best way I can explain it is the supervisors help people get in touch with just about everything in their lives that was difficult or painful and they help the candidates put it all into perspective. The theory is you cannot

60

be with other people in their pain, if you can't be with yourself *in your own*. Sounds confusing, but it's absolutely right. It was a difficult program for me. Getting close to the brokenness in your life is never an easy thing, especially if one has been through something unimaginable at an early age. Thanks to continued counseling when I returned to seminary in my junior year, I managed to work through some issues.

There was one comical thing that happened at the end of the CPE program. There was a final retreat day that took place at the summer home of the Sisters of the Sacred Heart in Nanaquaket, RI. This order of nuns taught me at Holy Ghost Grammar School. We used to have summer picnics here with the whole school...it was a beautiful place. I hadn't thought about that in many years. As we approached the facility, I began thinking: *Now, what are the odds I would meet a nun who would remember me?* Zero, of course, but that wasn't to be. When I arrived the first day, we were met by a dozen nuns! And they looked very different from my past. In grammar school the nuns had only their faces visible, in black from head to foot, except for a little brim of white framing their faces that looked like the white uneven paper in the bottom of a cookie package! Many years later, there they stood— short dresses, short veils with hair visible. A little shocking at first glance.

Anyway, as we approached the little group, one of the nuns looked at me as if she knew me. "Are you Elizabeth Lane?" she said. I thought I was going to throw up! These nuns knew why we were there; we were all Episcopalians! Yikes!! Was she going to pronounce a public excommunication on me? Turns out, she was the principal when I was in grammar school. There was a little small talk before we went about our business of the day. Ironically, I ended up having lunch seated right next to her! And even crazier, I was okay with it. She seemed very nice, not at all like I remembered as a child. She had a lot of questions and seemed genuinely happy for my choice. For some reason, as I was praising the church I was now a member of, I blurted out: "I didn't know God loved me until I was 31 years old." It was relevant to the conversation, but I'm sure it sounded a little harsh. Sister looked intently at me. I thought I detected a tear in her eye and she said, "We didn't teach you that, did we." I think that was a learning moment for her, as well as a healing moment for me.

Back to the letter I had written to the COM... I wrote about my grade improvement as well as my increased self-confidence. I also wrote about the possibility of going on the seminary-sponsored trip to Israel and that because of the trip, I might not be able to attend the required overnight April COM meeting. Anyone who was to make the trip to Israel would be taking early finals, so there would be a schedule conflict. I was assured by the chair of the COM that it wouldn't be a problem.

The meeting was early in the second semester. I found myself sitting with a group of individuals whose simple presence made me very uneasy. There were lots of questions that had little to do with my becoming a candidate...was it wise to consider a month-long trip since the last grades they saw weren't the greatest...I explained that the trip was a learning experience, that it was intended to be a pilgrimage, a study trip that would enhance my ministry.

All of a sudden a question came out of no where. A deacon on the COM asked, "What's your social issue?" *What???* Did I *have* to have a social issue? Apparently I was supposed to have one, and I failed that question. I froze except to say that I was scheduled to be taking a course in Bioethics and I was looking forward, for one thing, to learn more about end-of-life decisions.

I often felt cornered in these meetings which made me go blank, feeling unqualified and just plain stupid. I never was able to stand up for myself in anything...*even* in my personal life. If I *ever* needed self-confidence, the time was now, and it wasn't to be. Next they asked me to give them a passage in the Gospel of John that spoke to me. "What does it mean when you say that God is in control?" was the kicker. I said that 'cutting the corners off the puzzle pieces to make them fit' used to be my mode of operation until I learned that I just needed to trust God and he would prevail. "If God is in control," said another priest, "how do you explain Bosnia?" The expression on my face surely said "*Really???*" I pulled myself together and said that wasn't God's doing. I talked about the fallen human condition, sin, and that I could no more explain that than I could explain the death of a child to its mother. I didn't dazzle them with answers, but since the two "prickly" people on the COM didn't say anything, I thought I was okay. But I wasn't...

Much of the following is taken from my journal entries. Some I've tried to reconstruct; some is the journal entry itself, which I will identify. It might be a boring read, but it's what happened... and much of it isn't pretty...

On Sunday night Dan left me a message on the answering machine. We connected on Monday morning. He told me that the COM had decided not to vote on my candidacy. They wanted to "hold me over" until April, if I decided to come! *What on earth did that mean...if I decided to come?* It's amazing to me how a dozen people would even think I would scrap the last twelve years of my life without a fight! But, wait, there's more. Dan said the COM had three issues from our January meeting. First, he said they were left scratching their heads, wondering why I couldn't come up with one social issue. My response to Dan was that my issue was around sexuality and how we needed to learn to respect one another, but that I was afraid to bring it up. I told him that I freeze in those meetings and that I was intimidated by the deacon who seemed to be attacking me. Next, he said that they couldn't understand why I chose such an obscure passage in John when John is so packed with other things. Again, I said I froze and that what I said was in my mind because of a recent exam. "It all makes sense now," he said, understanding why my answers seemed so short. Lastly, he said that the COM said I had a lack of passion. Now I had to say, *"Really!!!???"* "What is their definition of passion?" I said. Should I have been banging on the table or raising my voice? He didn't say much about that. He said not to worry, that many people are held over, and that I would be considered again in April, if I chose to come. Again, that phrase...*if I chose to come.* I asked what he meant. He said they knew that it would be tight, what with the trip, exams, paper, and end of semester stuff, so they were leaving it up to me whether or not I came to the meeting. I said, "Don't you have to be a candidate for a year?" to which he replied, "Absolutely." "So then," I said, "I *have* to come to the meeting if I want to be ordained after graduation," to which he replied, "Well, that's up to you." It was like a bad movie. We hung up...I cried. Where was redemption in all this?

I returned to VTS in the afternoon of the 17th instead of the evening. At my mailbox I ran into a senior Ray Walden and we had a conversation about our meetings with our respective COMs. A member had said to him, "How are you going to feel when we turn you down for candidacy?" an" before Ray knew what he was saying, out of his mouth came, "You can't, because God has called me!" H" was told later that that was the turning point of his interview. *Oh, to be that bold!*

About an hour later at the monthly Healing Service I told Jane Morse, the officiant, that I had just returned from COM, that the Standing Committee had been cancelled, and that I was angry and hurt. She lay hands on me and prayed that the Holy Spirit would heal these hurts, suggesting that so much pain is sometimes caused in our church all in the name of God. Walking back to the dorm after the service two other students talked about their experiences. Back in my room I got a call from Amy, the fiancée of one of my friends, who talked a lot about how she communicates with clients. She was a representative for the Discover TV channel. It was a great practical conversation. That evening one of the younger students Heather Back and I went out for dinner, and she relayed an experience of her own that was painful.

After dinner I received a phone call from my oldest son Christian who also had lots to say about dealing with people who intimidate. Lots of little tidbits to help with the healing. God's presence was surely known.

Wednesday morning at Eucharist the sermon spoke to me of our enormous God who could transcend anything; it was the Feast of the Confession of St. Peter. Following a moving lecture on Martin Luther, I headed out to Herndon for a meeting with my field parish rector Brad Rundlett. After telling him about what happened he told me his story which was far worse than mine. He was very encouraging. After dinner that evening I had a wonderful talk with another friend Marty Bastian who shared his COM experience and we prayed together. He reminded me that I was pleasing God and *not* man and that all this pain would make me stronger, and make me dependent on God and *not* on pleasing or being accepted by the COM. He made a lot of sense. Later on that evening I received a call from Jane Morse asking if I would like to have lunch with her to talk about what had happened to me. So much encouragement, so much support. God was leading me through a thicket, but I wasn't alone.

It was the end of January 1995. My Advisee Group had a suggestion regarding my April visit with the COM. "Send them

64

your sermons, your CPE evaluation, and your Field Education evaluation. Maybe even some of your tests." Sounded like a good idea. It would give them an true picture of who I really am. My colloquy mentor Sam Walker offered to write a letter for me. When I mentioned this idea to Brad, he too wrote a letter of recommendation for me.

That evening I decided to call Garland first and tell him what I was planning to do. I told him I trusted him and wanted to know what happened at their last meeting. Some of what Garland told me was different from what Dan had indicated. He said that four persons on the COM were supportive of me while the others thought my academics weren't good enough. Interestingly though, Dan had never mentioned academics to me. And apparently my supposed "lack of passion" never came up at any meeting. It's very disconcerting when those people who have your life in their hands can't seem to be truthful.

While most people thought contacting all the COM members was a good idea, Lorne's response was the most helpful. He suggested that I call Dan and tell him I wanted to contact the other members and go with what he said. He also suggested that it sounded like the devil was using elitism to keep me out.

Richard Singleton was another ray of hope in this mess. He said that some people had an agenda and he wasn't happy about it. He said he felt they thought I didn't "fit the mold", that my grades weren't good enough, that I wasn't elite enough, proper enough, poised enough, etc., that I hadn't grown, and, in his words, he felt they thought I was a "ditsy blonde." Blonde, blue eyes and cute aren't assets in the priest business. Interestingly enough, since I didn't do anything at the meeting to cause them to see me as "ditsy", it truly is an agenda, a ploy to keep me out, particularly since I'm not politically correct.

I went to see Brad after that phone call. We prayed as we usually did and Brad's prayer was as if he knew what was on my heart. I dissolved in tears and told him what had happened. He was furious and said, "Of course you don't fit the mold! Praise God! It's time for a reformation!" We talked about that mold, what I'm not and what I am. At some point during the conversation I realized something very important. As much as I've tried to be comfortable in those meetings, I'm not. And consequently I've had to do everything twice. As I see it it's because my unconscious self, in an effort to protect myself, causes me to act in a way that's not comfortable for me, but (interestingly enough) is the proper, demure person they claim *they* want to see. And yet they're still not happy!

> *Not to us, Lord, not to us but to your name*
> *be the glory, because of your love and faithfulness.*
> Psalm 115:1

As I continued to plow through my feelings, God continued to speak to me through many people. Mary Wilson suggested that I should focus in on me and not them. Professor Bill Stafford didn't feel they asked any unacceptable questions and he suggested three things: learn to be articulate; clarify my vision; get a social issue! Give them my vision of what I would do in a parish. What touches my heart? What makes me sad? What gives me joy? (He agreed with me that I made the right decision not bringing up the "loafed" sexuality issue.) It didn't take but a minute for me to say that my social issue revolves around children and the family system. He asked me to elaborate. I said it comes from my own pain, a dysfunctional family, dealing with my own children's pain in divorce, parishes that don't want children in their services, etc. Bill's response was, "Well, there you have it. A social issue!" I told him when I had been asked the question I thought the deacon wanted something MAJOR! Of course Bill said, "Aren't families and children of major importance?" He was right. And I realized that in my effort to second-guess the question and talk about Bioethics which I hadn't even taken yet, I didn't sound genuine and they saw right through it. Sure I'm still angry, but I want to look at this in a positive way. I'm going to focus on me, present ME, and try to overlook the committee personalities.

Well, I received a letter yesterday from Dan saying he had made a mistake in telling me that April would be candidacy. He said the COM wanted to wait until June. My first read of that was negative—that they were jerking me around…again. My next read was that they want to wait for my full year grades. That made me angry. Chris' response was that it would take the pressure off April and allow me to be more relaxed. Maybe that might help.

Following CPE (Clinical Pastoral Education), I had begun counseling with Randall Prior, the rector of a church in Virginia. My CPE supervisors thought I would benefit if I continued with the work I had begun during CPE. Boy, were they right! It was interesting, informative, painful; that about sums it up. I had to learn to claim me, to claim the same messages I sent to others. Learning to have the courage of my convictions was a tall order for me, but if I expected to practice with authority, I had work to do. Nothing magical happens at ordination; what I was then is what I would be after ordination. As we peeled back the onion, as they say, it was amazing what we found, and what needed to be changed!

Ash Wednesday, March 1, 1995 at St. Timothy's in Herndon, VA. It was an experience like no other. Brad's focus was a reading from Corinthians: "You have received the grace of God; do not let it go for nothing." He said that he hated this day because it's a day where we are reminded that we are sinners and that we are going to die, that someday we're going to lose someone we love, that we may not always have tomorrow to say I'm sorry or I forgive you, and finally that we might not always have tomorrow to say I love you. It was very moving. I did the Imposition of Ashes with Him. After he blessed the two containers of ashes, he knelt beside me and I imposed ashes on his forehead. I felt really uncomfortable—my priest kneeling before me, the entire congregation watching, I didn't make a very good cross, but when I went to the rail and imposed ashes on those people, I was almost overcome with the power of the moment. Here were all types of people, most perfectly well, some sick, some old, some young, adults, children. And as I went from person to person I felt humbled and honored to be able to participate in this service. I felt blessed and most importantly, I felt called to do this. I thanked Brad later for allowing me the privilege of sharing in this ministry with him.

The Rev. Brad Rundlett
St. Timothy's, Herdon, VA.

I found the following journal entry connected to this night. The depth of what I wrote startled me, even after all these years, particularly since I sometimes wrote as if I was talking to God...

Journal Entry: 9:45am session. *Most holy and gracious God, "beloved of my heart"...that's what Brad called you on Monday— beloved of my heart. . .it has haunted me since then, the closeness, the intimacy, the depth of such an address...*

Feeling that unity with you is what I live for. You are indeed beloved of my heart as well. And it is that closeness, that intimacy that allows me to continue on this path you have chosen for me, cost what it may. And right now, as I see it, the cost is very high. How long will it be before I can really know and really accept who I am?

You have made me a woman, an attractive woman by most standards, that makes me appear younger than I really am, that sometimes evokes "cutesy" words. You have given me a happy, pleasant personality that sometimes makes me appear ditzy, and yet I wouldn't have it any other way. You have given me eyes to see you in the world. I take great joy in your creation, in nature, in the sky, in family. You have given me an inquisitive mind that, from the moment I knew you loved me after Cursillo 18, I wanted to know all there was to know about you. I wanted to learn who you were. You see, up until then you were in a classroom, in books, around corners waiting for me to sin. You were all too real, but in a negative way. Maybe that's why prayer is my lifeline, because you are truly real to me now and I will never lose that connection again. But I discovered my limitations early on.

Formal learning for me is very hard. It isn't so much that I can't understand, but that I must have an attention deficit, since I fall asleep so often and get distracted so easily. Whatever it is, it hasn't been easy. As I said, the price is high. But more importantly, you have given me a heart to know and love you, a heart that overflows with love for you. Even as I write those words my whole body tingles with the presence of you. You have set my heart on fire with flames that can never be quenched. A priest I am because I can be nothing else. There is nowhere else to go. Yet Roy's words ring in my head, about discernment and testing. But I know sure as I am sitting here that my call is to ordination. The road, however, is much more complicated than I ever dreamed.

You have given me gifts to carry out this ministry. Do I know what they are? Perhaps not all of them. I am a people-person. I am compassionate, loving, caring, insightful, intuitive. I can and have lead people to you, something that I cherish. Blessed and most holy God, draw me closer to you, so close that we touch in a way that I have never experienced before. Make today into a powerful experience. Show yourself to me, Lord. Let this day be a sign of my covenant with you and yours with me. Fill me with your peace.

Most holy and precious Jesus, we, you and I, reached a new level of intimacy today. We touched uncharted territory together. Fill all the spaces of my life to overflowing. Set my heart on fire with your passion this Lent that I may continue to know you in ways that are new and untouched."

April 23—25, 1995. C.O.M Candidacy Meeting. I was looking forward to and dreading this at the same time. I was totally unaware of how absolutely terrible this experience would be...Sunday afternoon to Tuesday lunch, talking, worshipping, and taking Old and New Testament canonicals. These tests were extra diocesan requirements above and beyond the seminary GOEs (General Ordination Exams). A little overkill, but there was no choice. Last week I had sent each member of the commission a package which contained: two Church History papers (both Graded "B"), an Ethics paper on Homosexuality (Grade "B"), newsletter articles that I had written for St. Timothy's Newsletter, fall semester sermons, Brad's fall semester evaluation, spring semester sermons, spring semester evaluation, and lay committee end-of-the-year evaluation.

When I arrived on Sunday several of the lay people on the committee thanked me for the package, saying they appreciated the effort and that they were glad to have the information. Monday morning, I took both canonicals and I felt good about them. We had informal group meetings all day and Monday evening I was told that the commission wanted to meet with me for a half hour to see how I was doing. I walked into the meeting and was blind-sided by Russ Ruffino, the rector of St. Peter's, Narragansett. He spoke in a progressively agitated fashion for at least fifteen minutes. "Your church history papers didn't make any sense to me and they were far below the B grade that you received... they were not written in an academic fashion. The homosexuality paper was unintelligible and definitely below the B grade that you had received. It was also poorly written, not logical, etc. etc. etc." But wait, there's more! He said on several occasions that I wasn't Anglican, that much of my writing sounded like dualism (God being distinct from creation); that God and mankind are against each other, and on, and on, and on! Again he said that he was concerned for the future church, that I didn't cut it academically, and that GOEs would eat me up in January. I thought I couldn't handle any more. I was wrong...he saved the most painful for last. He said that my sermons were shallow, not much in the way of teaching, that they appealed to emotions and sentiment and they weren't good.

I remember exactly how I felt at that moment, even these many years later. I didn't want to break down, but I didn't know how I was going to control my emotions. I'd never been attacked in such a way before, and I was afraid to respond. But it wasn't over yet. One of the deacons on the commission jumped in and said she agreed with Russ' comments on dualism, that I seemed to place mankind against God, that I talked too much about God's control over us, etc. The tears began to flow; I sat stoic and shocked, waiting for an opportunity to speak—*if* I was able to speak at all. When I did speak I basically said that I couldn't speak to the grades because grades were subjective, but that my professors were pleased and so was I. I said that we had been down the academic road before and I wasn't going to do it again. I said that I do the best I can, will continue to do the best I can, and that the important thing is to use the gifts I have been given. I said that I had no idea what Russ was talking about regarding dualism and that I was shocked at his comments. Then, finally, a supportive comment broke in. Richard Singleton, dean of the Cathedral, spoke to my Palm Sunday sermon, one that I had sent to the group. "Russ, what did you think of her Palm Sunday sermon?" Russ' comment: "shallow, emotional..." Richard said he thought it was "right on." A little ray of hope...but it wasn't enough.

> *Your word is a lamp unto my feet,*
> *a light unto my path.*
> Psalm 119:105

I don't remember a lot of what I said after that because I was shattered. It became obvious that this was a lose-lose situation; nothing I could possibly say would make any difference. Finally, I was asked the question: "If we don't make you a candidate for Holy Orders, what will you do?" Only God could have kept me from dissolving at that moment. Then, I spoke: "All I can say to you is that God has called me, it has been affirmed by VTS, and very much affirmed by my field ed parish, and if I *could* do anything else, I surely would because I don't need this!"

I left the room in tears after almost an hour. Both Richard and Dan came looking for me some time later. They said I had handled myself extremely well under such a heavy attack. *Really?* Is that a compliment or the beginning of the end? I learned much later that my canonicals were fine. I heard it from a mentor, but it was never mentioned during the meeting.

Even decades later, as I sit here and write these words, it's mind boggling that such an experience had occurred in the name of God. Such hurt, such injustice. But if I believed God was in control, it wasn't up to me as to how this would all work out. He had a plan, and I had to wait.

Friday, June 9, 1995 C.O.M Meeting. I returned from the Holy Land last week and preached on Sunday at St. Timothy's. It was wonderful to be back. Again faced with a COM meeting, Roy and I arrived in a positive mode. While we were waiting for one of the members to arrive, Dan asked me about my trip. I told him "one story." (That was the advice of our lecturer in the Holy Land— that we only tell <u>one</u> story.) I talked about my experience of riding on the back of a camel up Mt. Sinai...at 3am. An amazing experience! The members came in and Dan formally began the meeting.

I should have seen it coming. My conservative views, my evangelical style, my need to bring Jesus twelve inches south—head to heart—wasn't what they wanted in the Rhode Island churches, or maybe just within this small group in authority. A week later, I received a phone call: the recommendation was to defer my VTS senior year and to do an intern year with my parish priest. They wanted me to *not* return to seminary in September, but to spend that year "working on my formation" at a church in Rhode Island. I was speechless. *"Lord, you put this call into my heart 11 years ago. You've lead me every step of the way. Whenever I was unsure, you would somehow make it very clear what I was to do. You must do that now. I have to know and I have to feel you in this decision."*

What was I going to do? What would a sabbatical year look like? What about looking for another diocese? Why was there so much mistrust in the diocese? Even if I could answer those questions, I couldn't bear the thought of losing my VTS community or putting my St. Timothy community on hold. Thankfully, I was reminded of the three principles necessary when making a Christian decision:

1. Is my decision biblical?
2. Do circumstances make it possible?
3. Do I have God's peace when making this decision?

Certainly ordination and service to God is biblical. As I looked at the decisions I could make, the only one that didn't need a great deal of manipulation on my part is the decision to accept their proposal. That's not saying there isn't a lot of pain involved, but God can bless and honor pain and work through it. If the COM has made a mistake, God and I will triumph in the end. And there's the last thing—do you have God's peace? Strangely enough, looking at the third principle, existing on the verge of emotional exhaustion, I could feel God's presence, his comforting presence around me, holding me in my pain. It felt like the beginning of peace. I knew what I was going to do.

A week passed and I learned from a supporter that the Standing Committee didn't know I wasn't coming to the Standing Committee Meeting until I didn't show up! Manipulation and underhandedness had a free hand in the diocese at that time, said my supporters. Still nothing could be done to stop the wave that was crashing over me.

72

Meetings, and more meetings. Drafting letters, getting advice. My head was spinning. *God, how can this be happening?*

I had stopped writing quite some time ago. I don't know why...perhaps I've been very busy, but, more than likely, it's been difficult to dredge up the "process." That's what the church calls *all* the 'hoops' from the time a person talks to their rector and tells them they believe they have a call, to becoming a candidate for Holy Orders. I had some vivid memories of certain things, but when I got into my journals and read those things I'd forgotten, I found myself almost in a state of depression. God has a way of sometimes making you forget those things that are most disturbing or painful. My journals, however, brought it all back.

As I've said all along, all that we go through makes us who we are today. I guess it was all necessary to bring me to where God wanted me to be. But it wasn't fun! It's also difficult to turn journal entries into an easy read. I did my best in the previous section, and I'll do the same in the next section.

So, let's delve back into the abyss with a combination of writing and journal entries.

Thursday, July 13, 1995. I called Gary today and told him about yesterday's meeting. Gary still feels that things aren't right and he assured me that the Standing Committee will do all they can to "reconstruct" the Commission On Ministry when it's time to appoint new members in November. He also said that if Bishop Wissemann wants him to get involved on my behalf he would gladly support him. He said he affirms my going back to school.

I had lunch with Garland today. (Garland Teasley...a very sweet man who was gladly approaching retirement). Garland's take on yesterday was mixed. He didn't seem to agree with Russ' interpretation of the meeting the COM had before they met me in April. Garland said he couldn't understand why Russ seems to have so much power over the COM. When I told him I thought I

73

was going to go back to school, he said that he felt it was the right decision and that he supported it. In hindsight, while any amount of support would appear to be the light at the end of the tunnel...that light was actually the train, and it was headed straight for me. *Are you there, God? Are you still in control, God?*

> *"Let anyone who is thirsty come to me, and let the one who believes in me drink.*
> *As the scripture has said, '*
> *Out of the believer's heart shall flow*
> *rivers of living water.'".*
> John 7:37-38

Tuesday, July 18, 1995. Today I met with Bishop Wissemann. I gave him an overall picture; he read the proposal in my folder along with my middler evaluation. (I found it interesting that one of the two things he read was my evaluation; Dan had said the COM doesn't put much stock in an evaluation!) His first response was how was this proposal going to effect my family's financial situation. I thanked him for thinking of that because no one had asked me that question and it certainly has to be a consideration. From there we discussed the pros and cons of both decisions and the risks involved in each. He asked if I felt that there was a "hidden agenda". I mentioned the perception that I'm traditional, evangelical, and I wondered if the "baggage" of my former rector wasn't in play here. Lorne Coyle was possibly the only traditional, evangelical rector in the diocese who wasn't afraid to profess it. He shook his head as if he understood. He said there was another person who had a similar problem in the diocese. When I said I intended to write a letter to the COM telling them that I was going back to school, he felt that in my letter to the COM it would be a good idea to tell them why I came up with my decision, letting them know all my considerations.

Wednesday, July 19, 1995. I spoke to Gary this morning. He asked about my visit with the bishop. I said he was very nice and pastoral and I told Gary what we talked about. He said that Bishop Wissemann has been good for him in that he has been able to use him as a sounding board for all the things in the diocese that

74

have been getting on his nerves. Gary and I talked about the bishop's question regarding "hidden agenda." Gary said the truth was that if I was a "flaming, feminist, liberal lesbian" that the COM would be bending over backwards to help me through the process. But because I'm "the other", some of them had decided that the church has enough of them. Gary said that he has no intention of reappointing Russ to the COM in November. He also mentioned some trouble on the Continuing Ed Committee, that some people have resigned because of Russ.

I had lunch with Joan Lisi. I told her that Gary thought it would be a good idea to touch base with a lay member of the COM and that Joan was a "safe" person to talk to. We talked a lot about that idea, that a postulant has to be careful what they say and to whom and how she didn't think that was right or fair. I couldn't agree more. I told her a lot of what has gone on over the last few weeks. She said that Russ intimidates her and she thought the "hold" he has over the group isn't right. She said he seems to be a man that needs to be stroked. About Russ' comment that I only got through the process with a 4-3 vote, she said that was then and this is now, that they should be supporting me. When I mentioned Russ' comment about the meeting the COM had before the April meeting with me, she laughed as if she didn't agree with what he had said. Joan spent much time suggesting what I should say to the COM the next time I see them, how I need to uplift myself and "blow my own horn." She said that she could see no reason why the COM would be angry at my going back to school and doing the sabbatical year next year. All in all, it was a great lunch and I feel very confident with what she said.

Saturday, July 27, 1995. I sent a copy of the COM letter to Roy for final approval.

Dear Dan,

After much consideration, I am sending this letter in response to the 9 June meeting of the Commission on Ministry and their recommendation regarding my application for Candidacy for Holy Orders. Based on our phone conversation of 12 June and our meeting of 20 June, I have taken under advisement your comments and the concerns of the Commission. I have sought the counsel of many people, carefully weighing all that is involved, namely the academic, psychological, and emotional factors, along with my family's financial planning situation. After much prayer and deliberation, I have decided to return to school in September. I feel in my heart that an uninterrupted seminary education is the best way to continue my growth and formation at this time. With regard to the recommended sabbatical year I do feel that it would be an asset to my ministry and I would welcome the opportunity to continue working with Roy upon my return from seminary. I thank you and the Commission for all your efforts on my behalf and I look forward to seeing you again in April 1996. Please feel free to call me if more clarification is needed.

Sincerely in Christ,
Elizabeth L. Myers

CC: Roy and Gary

Not surprising, there was no response from the COM after they received my letter saying that I was returning to school.

The summer was almost over, and I couldn't wait to get back to seminary in September. With little understanding of how my future would turn out, my only option is to trust the One who has led me this far...

You might be wondering at this point about everything else in my life. To be honest, I remember little. This was a very frightening time in my life. Every day, every week, it felt like another piece of my life was disintegrating and I could do nothing to stop it. Chris visited about every six weeks. I went home on holidays. But my heart was in turmoil. Enough said...

Then came my senior year—1995—it was hard to believe. I remember walking around campus seeing the excitement of the juniors. They were beginning a wonderful chapter in their lives and hopefully, they wouldn't experience my journey!

We had a Quiet Day on October 3rd. led by the Dean Martha Horne. She brought us into the wilderness this morning. She spoke of the Israelites being in the desert, Jesus being in the desert, and us being in the desert we call "seminary." She referred to all three as being a place of testing and temptation, a place "in between" where we were and where we are going to be. She cautioned us to watch for demons—in ourselves, in other students, in faculty, and in my case I would add... in my diocese.

The next major event for me was the election of the new bishop in Rhode Island. Bishop George Hunt had retired and Bishop Wisseman had been an interim until the new bishop was elected. That happened in the late fall of my senior year. I wanted to put the hurts and fears of the past behind me and go forward. I'd hoped this would be the beginning of a new era for the diocese as well as for me.

Geralyn Wolfe was her name; she described herself as a liturgist, preacher, teacher, and spiritual guide. I remember reading her statements last month and not thinking much of her. She had strayed from the traditional way of presenting a resume. She mentioned nothing of her personal life, which made me suspicious. What does that say about her? I so often identify myself by my relationships to my family. What does that say about me? And yet, she was elected. I went back and reread the statements. I realized the strength in what she wrote. She knows who she is. It made me think . . . again: who am I? It caused me to decide to spend some of my Quiet Day analyzing, reflecting, and claiming who I am. I had to show a part of that person yesterday morning when I "celebrated" Eucharist in Liturgics Practicum; I had to show a part of that person yesterday afternoon in class when I did a role play—something I hate to do. I needed to assess who that person is again, give her some "handles", tell her that I love her, affirm her uniqueness. I don't think I've ever done that; but God does it all the time.

In mid February I sent a fax to Roy Greene, rector of Trinity Church, my home parish in Newport, Rhode Island. I was planning to go back home for the new bishop's consecration, but would be returning to seminary on Sunday. There would be no time to meet, so I sent him an update.

Dear Roy,

I'll be home Saturday for the consecration and returning on Sunday—a whirlwind visit—so we won't have time to talk, but I just wanted to write a few words to you.

Not a day goes by that I don't think about the April meeting; however, I'm thinking about it in a different way. Everything you and I talked about (the five issues) may indeed need to be put on the table, but I'm not sure I'm the one to do that. And neither are you. My history with the COM is that we have a meeting, little real helpful communication occurs, and I leave. I receive no written communication and I hear from one or two members (when I ask) just exactly how the COM feels. That's not communication, that's not the way to run a Christian gathering of any kind, and that is anything but encouraging.

I went in there last June wanting to wipe the slate clean and start fresh. I thought I handled myself well. I came away feeling hopeful, and the bottom fell out. What I'm saying is why should I be expected to tell them what I think their issues are with me? I am a strong believer in the hierarchy of the church, but this isn't hierarchy; this is abuse of power.

Why can't we speak truthfully and honestly with one another? Who better to answer their questions about me—than me? Why can't I simply say something like, "This is my third candidacy meeting, and our fourth attempt to work together toward my candidacy. There is a wall between us and we're not communicating. We both want the same things for the Church, so let's be open and honest with each other. Talk to me about what's on your mind and I'll do my best to answer your questions." To me that's the most helpful way I can handle it.

I have no doubt about my call. Yes, I'm different, and I'm beginning to thank God for that. Our Church is changing and if we don't start speaking directly to one another, we're going to destroy any sense of Christian love.

You and I talked about empowering vs. encouraging. I hope we can somehow start to look at each other in the present. I have grown and I'm quite frankly tired of the past hanging on unfairly. I want April to be a beginning, not a continuation. I'm willing to talk to them and be honest; they have to be willing to talk to me and be honest. I want to break the cycle; it's time.

I also would like to talk to the bishop when I'm home in March. She sent me a handwritten letter the other day (it was the first I'd heard about her pneumonia). It's no wonder seminarians *feel left out on a limb; it would have been nice if someone in the bishop's office let the seminarians know about her illness; we could have prayed for her! But that's just another example of the lack of Christian sensitivity and caring we have had in the places of power in our diocese. I'm not saying all these things in anger; I say them with great concern and pain. This wasn't what Jesus had in mind. The early church held all things in common. They didn't just break bread together. They showed real care for each other in Christian love. Why can't we do that?*

I'll see you on Saturday. My plane gets in at 9am and Chris will pick me up and we'll go over to the Convention Center. When Dan was down here last week I asked about Judith Davis and the planning of the ceremony, telling him that I had offered my services to Ron Crocker at Convention, but had heard nothing. He suggested I call her. I did and she basically said that there really wasn't anything I could do but that the seminarians could be part of the procession, and, by the way, bring my alb! Another example of the wonderful communication we have. If I hadn't called her, I would not have known to bring my alb home and would not have been in the procession.

I hope your presence in our diocese as a caring pastor and the spirituality of our new bishop will be enough to turn around a diocese that needs a wake-up call.

Thanks for being there.
In His name,
Elizabeth

PS. Commencement plans are beginning and tickets are being given out. It's Thursday, May 16th at 10am. If you plan to come, please let me know.

A few days later, I received an e-mail from Lorne....

I found you in my prayers this morning. How did you do on GOEs? What is happening in RI with your candidacy? How are you? I am missing you and need to know how to pray. Can I help in some other way?
In His love, Lorne

Oh, how I needed that! Short...sweet...all I need. That's the kind of support a seminarian is supposed to get from her rector and her diocese! Lorne had been called to Trinity, Vero Beach, Florida, shortly after I left for seminary. It was so nice to hear from him.

My response:

Lorne-

God certainly is good to put me into your prayers today. GOE results arrived on Monday and I did not do well as far as the 7 areas are concerned. The readers' comments, for the most part were about 50-50. They said my answers were "OK" "adequate" "off the mark", etc. There were as many good comments as there were criticisms. But the bottom line, for them, was there wasn't enough in each area to satisfy them. It was difficult on Monday to see an occasional classmate with a big smile on his or her face. Interestingly enough, I felt a sense of peace on Monday. I know God has called me to be a priest and this is just another situation I have to deal with. Chris, on the other hand, is so frustrated, not knowing what to say or do. He's having trouble with the idea that the readers don't tell you what the "right" answer would have been.

Yesterday was a regroup day for me, getting about the busyness of things…but today…you know me…I've always needed a good cry to get on with things. Interestingly enough, you sent your e-mail at 11:50am and no more than 15 minutes later I was in tears with a friend of mine. God is good. When we pay attention to each other, he can certainly use us to help one another. The tears were frustration over this whole process, anxiety over what happens next… just a general "I'm tired of all this." I'm meeting with the new Bishop on Tuesday. (Next week is spring break.) I have a good gut feeling about her; I hope I'm not disappointed again. I have a meeting with Roy on Tuesday afternoon and I'm supposed to have another candidacy interview during the April overnight at ECC. Right now I'm sorting out things that need to be said to the COM in April. It's going to be difficult to be myself, which is obviously threatening to some of them, and at the same time do what I can to make the process into "community." Knowing that you pray for me means more to me than you'll ever know. There's nothing you can do for me as far as the diocese is concerned. But who knows what the future will bring! Thanks for caring.

In His love,
Elizabeth

A response from Lorne that evening…

Elizabeth –

Amazing "coincidence", that our Lord should have made me pray for you today! Actually, I thought of you last week but only shot up an "arrow prayer" for you since it was in the middle of the workday. Today I was in the midst of a prayer of adoration when the Spirit interrupted me and reminded me of you, that how you needed my intercession and His care. So, who can disobey that?

I'm sorry to hear of the GOEs. Those results will not help your case. However, a caring COM/Bishop can choose to have you make up the deficits in other ways, such as continuing ed. Courses, reading, mentoring with someone learned, etc. All is not lost; in fact, all shall be well. I'd guess it's just Chris' "green" (Myers-Briggs) that makes him want to know the right answer when the only right answer you want to hear (from anyone) is, "I love you and I'm sorry for this crap".

I talked at length with Fr. Ostman in Newport yesterday on a common pastoral emergency. When that was done, he actually said he had some hope for the new bishop and that he felt she was really the most moderate of the nominees. So I'll be praying that her attitude with you is one of "how can I help you get qualified?" and not "how can I get rid of you?"

Love, Lorne

As I read my journal entry for the meeting with Geralyn, I already knew what it said. It is one of the few events in my process that I'll never forget. As I think about it all now, there were so many times along the way that I felt so inadequate, and so many people in authority who were supposed to lift me up, did exactly the opposite. The meeting with the bishop was no different…

We met on March 5th and there was small talk for a short while. Then, without warning, there was an invasive spiritual direction session.

Bishop: "What sustains you through this process?"
Answer: *"I think of Peter. He was unpredictable, sometimes unsure, close to Jesus."*

Bishop: "What biblical story do you connect to?"
Answer: *"The Transfiguration."*

Bishop: "Who are you in the story?"
Answer: *"John."*

Bishop: "What are you doing?"
Answer: *"I am on the ground in fear and awe."*

Bishop: "What is the fear about?"
Answer: *"I don't know—perhaps that I won't get ordained."*

Bishop: "OK. I'm no longer Geralyn; I'm Jesus. I say, 'Don't build booths.' Now what are you going to do?"
Answer: *"I weep. I'll go back down the mountain; I'll bring Christ's love to all I meet; I'll be Christ's presence; I'll serve."*

Bishop: "That's bunk! That's intellectualizing. Don't think so hard. What are the tears about? As you read scripture over the next few weeks, combine your tears with the tears of Jesus and Mary. Look at the tears. What do they say? How are they like those who wept in Scripture?"

That was the extent of my interview with the Bishop. When I left, I remember thinking 'what was that all about?' I still don't know. If I was ever worried about my future—if I ever thought God was absent—this definitely was the time!

I went to my Concordance. I looked up references to **tears, cry,** and **weep.** Didn't matter, because I had no answers or understanding. What on earth was she trying to get out of me?

I met with Roy the next day. I told him of my visit with the bishop. He wanted to know why I was talking about that instead of talking about my GOE results! He said I seemed to be "all right"… but how could I be all right with such results! I went back and forth with emotional ups and downs throughout this process and, I guess, why should this day be any different? I said

I was devastated, but what was I supposed to do, cry all the time. I do enough of that! He asked what I did when I got the results. I said I looked at them and put them back in the envelope and went to class. I said I didn't really look at them closely until I came home. He couldn't understand that. I said that Bishop Mark had said that four days of tests didn't cancel out 2½ years of education and experience. God bless Bishop Mark Dyer, one of my favorite professors! He taught me the importance of sensitivity, love and trust. Bishop Mark's response didn't make Roy happy because he interpreted that to mean that we were blowing off GOEs. At one point I finally asked whether I still had his support. He said if I felt I had a call he would support me. I sent an e-mail to Lorne. Thankfully he was supportive and understood...*you are experiencing things as Job did... they would probably be happy if you excused yourself from the process... don't let them off the hook. God has called you, not them, and His Church has already affirmed that call in a number of ways...*

The Rt. Rev. Mark Dyer
A professor and one of my biggest supporters

He suggested that I read an article entitled <u>Two Churches in the Episcopal Church</u>, written by Bishop MacNaughton. The "other" church is evangelical, charismatic, and conservative, which he thought might be the opposite of my rector and my new bishop. He even offered to send me a copy of the requirement in the Diocese of Central Florida. Little did I know... He ended his email with: "I continue to pray for you. You are a valuable, worthy, spiritual servant of Jesus."

Back in seminary in March, it was an effort to immerse myself in my senior year, with all the surrounding issues. But God managed to keep me afloat...

On March 20th, there was a Community Healing service with Communion. I was asked a month ago by the Worship Committee to be one of three standing at three healing stations. Since I had begun weekly healing services at the seminary, the staff obviously appreciated my efforts. It was the first time a non-cleric had been asked to do this at VTS. The letter said it was in recognition of my healing ministry here at VTS. I tried to learn the 'generic' prayers, but it didn't seem right. *Lord, you'll give me the words..."* So with fear and trembling, at the appointed time, I approached the kneeler and the people came: students, professors, spouses... even *my* professors: Burt Newman, Bishop Mark—they came to *my station.* My knees were shaking but the words came: *"Gracious and holy God: send your Spirit... strengthen... above all let your servant know he is a treasured child in your kingdom..."* It was powerful, affirming, encouraging.

I sat in the chapel the next day with Psalm 69: "Save me, O God, for the waters have risen up to my neck . . . I have grown weary with my crying... those who hate me without a cause..." I thought of my Old Testament canonicals last year...*psalms don't mean anything*, they said. Psalms didn't mean anything? I wondered how many psalms come from tears; it seemed like more than less.

Professor Jim Ross who had just lost his wife preached an incredible sermon on this psalm. He said that his ministry is from tears and pain. He made one statement that I'll never forget. He said, **"I've been to the bottom...and it holds!"** He talked of detachments and not showing feelings, and he spoke of AA meetings. He said, "I should have known that the Bible itself gives us full permission and even encourages us to express our feelings openly." And then he said it finally dawned on him, after teaching it for years, that the Book of Psalms "in spite of its name—Praises—has more laments and outpourings of grief than it does songs of thanks." He answered my questions without knowing it. The psalmists cried—*I often cry*—I minister from pain. The realization brings me to tears. I couldn't sing the final hymn...one of my favorites: *Like the murmur of the dove's song, like the branches of the vine*...I can't sing and cry at the same time. For the rest of that month I read, I transcribed, I stressed, I worried, I prepared for April...I prayed.

The final meeting with the Commission on Ministry: April 14, 1996. So much writing and information to gather. For what??? I probably won't even get to offer any of it...

My background.

- 1983 to the present; it's a continual process.
- It's remaining open and faithful to God's grace and love through prayer, Scripture and community.
- It's knowing that being unworthy is precisely why he's given me this call because I am a wounded healer, to use Henry Nouwen's phrase.
- My life experiences have been my greatest gifts to others and I believe God will continue to use them in my ministry.
- Richard Capon wrote: "Priests are mirrors in which the church sees the priesthood it already has." To me that means the ordained person models ministry thus encouraging and supporting the laity in the use of their gifts for ministry.

My theology: What do I believe and practice?

- The creeds and the baptismal covenant framed in the double commandment of unconditional love. How? Ask what would Jesus do in this situation? That creates a tension between my unforgiving human nature and what I call my "homing device," the inner restlessness of spirit, which if I listen, continually calls me to greater heights which is reflected in first century preaching (e.g. Andrew of Crete, Jerome, John Chrysostom)
- Johannine Christology: God is in control; the revelation of the glory and mystery of God; "As the Father has loved me so I have loved you."
- Orthodox spirituality: It is a way of life. "One who practices Orthodox spirituality lives out a life of sanctification in the Sacraments, the Mysteries of God's continuing presence. Prayer and devotions come in and out of the liturgy. There is a companionship between Anglicanism and Orthodoxy because when we take our lives seriously as Anglicans, we have to say the same thing." (Bishop Mark Dyer)
- Evangelical: I believe in preaching the Gospel and upholding Scripture.

My view of mission and ministry
John 9, prayer, and liturgy

- *The man born blind is mission*: These are the people of God who need to hear and see the word of God preached and celebrated, whether they realize it or not. These are the people of God who have a void in their lives which they fill up with things of the world, but nothing can satisfy their restlessness of spirit. These are the wealthy, the marginalized, the educated, the simple, the adult, the child. We are the man born blind.

- *The man with his sight is ministry*: Having received his sight—a glimpse of the future kingdom—he can't help but preach it, regardless of the consequences, and inspired by the Spirit, he is bold for Christ and upholds the Gospel. We need to be the man who has regained his sight.

- My ministry is prayerful and contemplative because it is out of contemplative moments that I know who I am, from my baptismal covenant, and whose I am (1 Peter 1:2ff - chosen, destined by God the Father, sanctified by the Spirit to be obedient to Jesus Christ and to be sprinkled with his blood).

- My ministry at its best is under the model of ministry put forth by RC theologian David Tracy from the University of Chicago: Begin with experience which invites feelings. Then proceed to reasoned reflection, theological judgment, and then to action. In the Church today we more often go from feelings to action without proper thought and prayer.

- Mission and ministry begins with liturgy. Liturgy is the icon through which we see and experience God. Theology begins with liturgy. Therefore, when the faith community gathers for prayer, reading of Scripture, and breaking of bread, that is where ministry begins.

My strengths for ministry

- *Preaching, teaching, spirituality* and *pastoral ministry* are the strengths which are highlighted most often by those in my field parish. I preach once a month. I have been called a vulnerable preacher by many because I share my experiences, and I have been called a radical preacher because I'm not afraid to deliver a message that will give them something to think about. I have taught classes on prayer and spirituality which have proved to be powerful vehicles of God's grace in the lives of those who participated. My willingness to be vulnerable in preaching, teaching and relationships has allowed me to be more than an empathetic pastoral presence.

- A *pastoral presence* and *leadership ability* are those strengths for ministry most often recognized by the seminary community. I make an effort to be sensitive to what is going on around me. Because of that awareness, I have been a spiritual, prayerful presence to a number of people in a number of situations. During my seminary career I have organized weekly healing services and Lenten Taize Services which will be continued by juniors who have expressed an interest. During my three years I have also been the originator and coordinator of study notes for Church History, Liturgics, Ethics and Ecclesiology.

- I believe my pain keeps me human. Out of that pain comes a great sense of pastoral understanding of others in their pain which allows wonderful opportunities of growth in faith.

What is my vision of the future church?

- Return to the style of the early church and the Reformation Churches: Spirituality and prayer at the heart of ministry with the return of icon and symbol to enhance its liturgy. By that I mean attention needs to be given to the visual and audible elements of worship. Everything that deals with liturgy (e.g. worship space, "players", music, preaching, readings, officiating) must lift the congregation out of themselves giving them a glimpse of heaven. Ministry, theology, and spirituality begin with liturgy.

- We are going to have to reach people where they are. That may mean more evening opportunities for worship (e.g. Friday or Saturday). House churches will become more prevalent.

- Church leaders (e.g. vestries) must be transformed from governing boards into spiritual leaders. Congregations reflect their vestries. (See Transforming Church Boards by Charles M. Olsen, Alban Institute)

- Future clergy need to be more flexible and more adaptable ministry-sharers about the business of enabling congregations to discover their God-given talents. (See "It Is Time to Think New Thoughts" by Richard Kew and Roger White, *The Living Church*, January 7, 1996)

Be ready to talk about my decision to return to school last September vs. spending a sabbatical year at home.

Be ready to respond to my December letter about candidacy being denied again.

Weaknesses

- *Lack of confidence* in myself and those gifts which God has given me. When I think of Peter with all his faults and imperfections and how God used him to further His kingdom, I'm humbled that God has chosen me to follow Him. Indeed God often chooses the least among us. I also am aware that I can be *judgmental*, especially where I feel a passion on a particular subject. For example, I'm not very tolerant of people who don't understand the importance of the Christian community gathering together on Sunday morning to worship God when they'd rather be doing some other activity. Church membership and participation is not having your name on the parish register; it is hearing Scripture, receiving the bread and wine, and participating in the prayers. When I think of those who attend sporadically, I want to shake them and say: "Don't you understand that your lives could have so much more meaning if you became vulnerable and turned your lives over to the Lord?" And when I see them come to Church, my heart just aches for the sadness in their eyes, for the pain that I see at the altar rail. To combat my judgmental feeling and where the texts allow, I've worked the importance of community into sermons and conversations in a non-threatening way hoping to reach the ears of those who need to hear that message.

Formation

- Has only come up in the Church in the last few decades; definition varies depending on who asks the question; as a general rule can be defined as: the image of a priest
- 1 Sam.16:7: The Lord does not see as mortals see; they look on the outward appearance, but the Lord looks on the heart.
- Rom. 5:3f: Suffering produces endurance, endurance produces character and character produces hope and hope does not disappoint us, because God's love has been poured into our hearts through the Holy Spirit that has been given to us.

In all of this, I received some suggestions from Roy: Ask directly: You have a right to know what people are thinking; if you don't like the question, ask them to reframe it; if you think it's a loaded question, say so; ask them — what are your concerns?

At this point in my journal, I came to a startling discovery: the second most devastating event in my life, and I didn't record it...anywhere! Perhaps because I knew I'd never forget it, no matter where my journey led me. As I read over all the above notes, I was shocked at how I actually expected that I'd get to defend myself with all that I had written. But it wasn't to be. It was April 14, 1996. The meeting took place at ECC. The room was filled with clergy and lay persons; the entire COM was present. You could have heard a pin drop and the meeting was short and sweet.

If you recall, on the advice of my seminary professors, I had put together a package of sermons, graded tests, and recommendations from various professors. I had sent a copy to each member of the Commission weeks in advance; they were going to see exactly who I was, even if they weren't willing to ask me outright. A couple of the lay persons thanked me for sending the package. They said it was very informative and they appreciated the information. Then...just like that...the wheels came off the bus. A deacon made a negative comment about one of my papers, asking me how I could have possibly come to such a conclusion. I froze. Then the final blow came. Russ told me that my sermons were shallow, and that sending such a package to the COM was a bad idea. *I knew my sermons were good. I had watched the Spirit actually touch people when I preached.* This was more pain than I had ever expected. I tried to hold them back, but the tears just rolled down my checks. I had little fight left. I remember Richard Singleton's words — twenty-plus years later — like it was yesterday: "Elizabeth, what will you do if you don't get ordained?" In an instant, trying to hold back that I was falling apart, I said, "I have no idea, because nobody needs this!" And I walked out of the room. I have no recollection of what happened next, how I got home, or what the next few days were like. Obviously, I went back to school, in preparation for graduation. But then what? I didn't know.

A few weeks later I received a letter from Bishop Geralyn Wolfe. She requested that I attend a meeting in her office on May 11th— five days before graduation! She paid for the ticket. What choice did I have? Things were obviously coming to a head.

God always sends people to bring clarity to a situation. He did so the Sunday before my infamous meeting. Sitting down with a woman who was in pain...the sins of the parents being visited upon the children. Do I believe that? No, but it was the first thing that came to mind. What I heard was *my* hurt...a desperate, sickened child devastated over what she had done. The world isn't ours. It really is controlled or at least under the reign of the devil. He does "prowl around like a roaring lion, looking for some one to devour . . ." There is so much sin in the world. None is worse than the other. All sin is evil and tears at our souls. And there is something to be said for "he who is without sin cast the first stone." I told her to pray, to get back to church, to look at her life. And for me? Here I sit two days before my "summons" by the RI Bishop. Bishop Mark told me what to say—that I should ask them to judge GOEs *beside* my clinical (Field Ed and CPE) and my personal and spiritual growth. He also reminded me that if I was denied candidacy, they wouldn't be the last word. He said anyone who knows me knows I should be ordained and that I should let him and the faculty know if I come to a roadblock. Then he prayed and laid his hands on me in blessing. *Lord, help me to be firm, strong, faithful, and not afraid. Speak through me—think through me—set my heart on fire for your word, and your truth that I may guide those in my care.*

The day had arrived—May 11, 1996—the most humiliating, devastating day of my life. The players: Bishop Wolfe; Roy Green, my rector; Dean Singleton, COM member Sandra Haines, Chris and me. Before Chris and I entered the room we could hear laughter...about what...we would never know. But when I reached the door, all went silent. No welcome words, no prayer, just right to the business at hand.

We sat down and the Bishop spoke. "I'll get right to the point," she said, "the COM has made a recommendation and I concur. We are not giving you candidacy and we are dropping you from the process." It was as if someone had pounded a stake through my heart! Just like that, it was over; all those years of work flashed through my mind. *God, where did you go? Was I misinformed? Could I have been that misguided?* It was quiet for a moment, then I asked why. She said: "Your GOEs were weak, you don't have the grounding to be an ordained person, and you went back to school when the COM recommended that you not." Yes, I knew my GOEs were mediocre, but my professors had said those scores tell only part of your story. *And what on earth did she mean that I wasn't grounded enough to be ordained? And about finishing my third seminary year? It was a recommendation, not an order!* I knew it was all just a smokescreen for the *real* reason. Some words from Dean Singleton about my skills being effective in Cursillo, but it fell on deaf ears. Sandra Haines said that I ignored the new people on the COM, which was a crock; I had no idea what she was talking about. The Bishop said that she was able to make the decision to release me simply because "I don't know you." *How much sense does that make?* And not a word from Roy. Nothing. Chris had a few words with Singleton and Sandra, but it didn't matter. Somehow I managed to say that if there was no place for me in Rhode Island (which I knew was the real reason for my denial), perhaps there would be a place for me in another diocese. She somewhat agreed with that, but I'd have to pursue that on my own.

The rest of the day was a blur. My life was going up in smoke right before my eyes with Seminary graduation only a couple of days away!

The next day I returned to school for graduation on Thursday. I think I was numb for several months. But my friends were wonderful. Nancy, Bill, Judy, Marty, Alan, David, and many, many others came by my room just to give me a hug and express their anger. Even professors were upset and said they would do whatever they could to help. That indeed was comforting.

Graduation, however, was wonderful, even though I wasn't going to be ordained with a few weeks like almost all of my friends. Lisa, Ian, and Christian (II and III) were there. Chris and Diane couldn't come. Diane was pregnant and due any day. Roy was there because he had other business in Alexandria. Brad and Roger were there from St. Timothy's. It was a beautiful graduation, and if only for a few hours, I forgot all the pain that had brought me to this point in my life.

Graduation May 16, 1996

We left for home the next day. I had a lot of time on the drive home to wonder what was next. And the reason came rather quickly: my family needed me at that point in time; my situation would have to go on back burner. Lisa and 2-year old Ian moved in with us; she had left Paul and was looking for an apartment for them. She had decided to get a divorce from Paul. Shortly thereafter, Diane and Chris had Erin and a grandma was needed. And lastly, Jason was in jail in Pennsylvania for marijuana possession! *I get it, God; I was needed at home...but for how long?...*

CHAPTER 6

..... Back to 99 Cliff Avenue, Portsmouth, RI

A couple of months went by. I was lost. I felt God had abandoned me. I struggled back and forth between not caring and not praying to wanting that close feeling with God back again. One such night happened at St. Paul's Church in Portsmouth. I used to frequent the Wednesday night healing services. On this particular night the feeling of warmth returned. It had been *so long*. It wasn't there as hands were laid on me for Lisa and Paul, but it *was* there as I laid hands on someone else! *Am I being lead to more active service with Aaron in the healing ministry?* As I began to encounter God again, I listened more closely.

That same night Bishop Wolfe happened to be on television, talking with her doctors about her cancer treatment. I looked at her and thought, *I hope she beats the cancer, but I have little feeling for her.* In my talks with Aaron, he said he'd never met anyone with as deep a faith as she. Yet, he said she's also rude and cold. *Lord, give me the strength to go on, to find the answers, to hear you, to focus, to be helpful to Lisa and Paul, to read and catch up. Lord, continue to make me a priest in your church.*

A few months went by. When I did sleep, which wasn't much, I had these crazy dreams. The former RI Bishop George Hunt was celebrating the Eucharist. He served me the chalice in the front row, and he was telling me to get a vestment and serve with him. It was an unfamiliar church. I didn't know where the vestments were and when I finally found them, none fit—too small. No one would help me. George was waiting and I was crying...so frustrated. What did it all mean?

Meanwhile life went on without me, at least on the spiritual side. I spent a lot of time with Ian. That was a bright spot in an otherwise painful time. If Lisa was out, I had an opportunity to take care of Ian and I loved every minute of it. On one such night, Paul had called. Ian told him Lisa wasn't here. I don't know what else was said, but whatever was said, it was hard on Ian...it was hard on *all* of us. It felt like so many things in my life couldn't be fixed. There were times I just ached to be back in Virginia, where people knew who I really was... at St. Timothy's, ministering, pastoring, preaching, serving on the altar. It was almost September; I'd been home for four months now and I was forced to reevaluate my situation.

Thank goodness for Bishop Mark Dyer and Dr. Edward Kryder; they held me up when I couldn't manage myself. I had no motivation, no drive. I felt defeated, and yet I knew I needed to feel at home in church again. Bishop Mark wasn't surprised at how I was feeling. He said we all need goals—all humans do. I knew that, but I guess I was unable to be a good pastor to myself. I told him that I wasn't even motivated to pray; weekday and Sunday Eucharist, however, were bright spots for me. He said when we don't feel we can pray, it is *others* that hold us up—the fellowship of corporate worship. I tended to be so pessimistic about myself and my life. That's probably why I couldn't help myself. When I questioned Dr. Kryder if I should take GOEs again, his advice was, "Taking GOEs without having a supporting bishop could be misconstrued as manipulative." That was surely the last thing I needed.

The wonderful thing about choices and decisions is I always seemed to know when I'd received the right counsel...made the right decision. The strangest thing happened. Trinity's rector Roy Greene offered me a Pastoral Care chairmanship position. I felt it was like throwing me a bone. There was even one Sunday when there were three priests on the altar...and me, a chalicist...a token gesture at best. I wasn't really needed there. Nothing felt right.

Then the second crazy opportunity happened. My friend Anne Todd was Russ Ruffino's secretary at St. Peter's in Narragansett. It seems that their organist was leaving and they wondered if I could act as interim organist while they did a search! What on earth was Anne thinking? How could I possibly work for the man who did everything he could to see that I was dismissed by the Commission on Ministry? Could I work for him? I certainly could; I was qualified enough, but my fearful side tried to talk me out of it. I thought long and hard and I decided I'd do it. After all, it was a paying job, and all I could do was try.

A short amount of time went by. Taking the organist position would mean I would have little connection to Trinity, so I declined the Pastoral Care chairmanship. Thinking about it now, I can't imagine where I got the strength to accept such a position in the

94

first place. My drive was gone; my spirit was crushed. But for some reason, I forged ahead.

It turns out, as usual, God knew what he was doing. Like I say continually to my parishioners today, "God is in control; you are just along for the ride." Well, my ride, at this stage in my journey, was *more* than a wild ride. I should have expected what happened, but the truth is I was too far down to anticipate that the music would become my salvation and the beginning of my road back to the heart of God.

One day, in late September 1996, as I was driving to St. Peter's, thinking about what I was about to get into, I was listening to a cassette I hadn't heard in a long time: *Pieces of promises, parts of a prayer, No real commitment to stay or to care. Partly believing and partly in doubt, Not quite in the kingdom and not really out. Tied to your word, Lord, just by a thread, the need in my heart and the world in my head. So long in confusion that I couldn't see, Full time—not part time—it's you that I need.* I almost couldn't contain the tears! The refrain continued: *So Lord, come on in—'cause I want to start all over again. This day, all my life's an open door, I won't be your part time servant any more.* The second verse sealed the deal: *I've stayed on the fences, by the green hills, just on the edge of my world and your will. But now for the first time I know what to do, I'm ready—I'm coming—full time—to You!* There were still no answers to my ordination, but I knew this was the beginning of the path...the way back.

Music—prayer—for me there was no difference. Actually, there has *never* been a difference. I just never realized how important it would be for me some day. Right then, it was my salvation. It still brings me closer to God, closer than any other experience. It says what I feel. It puts words where I have none. I used to speak prayers, but not now. There's power in music. It reaches the depths of your very being when nothing else can. I believe God offered me this job not only to help St. Peter's (and get paid for it) but to strengthen my spiritual life. It even helped me get through degrading meetings with Russ. He actually talked to me as if I knew nothing about liturgy. He never mentioned my derailed journey, my seminary years, the COM meetings...nothing. It was as if the last twelve years of my life had never occurred. But the music...

In October of 1996 I returned to Virginia Seminary for the Annual Convocation. I had the opportunity to meet with several clergy who wanted to help me. Bishop Clay Matthews said that if I wanted to go to places like Nevada, West Texas, Colorado, or Michigan they would probably bend the rules regarding Canonical Residence, Postulancy and Candidacy. (In hindsight, that sounded like they were so hard up for clergy, they'd take anyone.) He said that Virginia wouldn't consider me unless I took GOEs again...*unless* I was fluent in Spanish and had a desire for rural ministry. *Really?* Thank God for Bishop Mark. He knew I had a call. But where will it bring me? And when will others see it?

Still going through my journal, and these so many years later, much of it doesn't make sense. In some places I don't even remember the conversations or notations! It's a little disconcerting to think I would forget, but as I think about it, perhaps "forgetting" is God's way of healing and protecting us from things that we don't really need to remember...

About that time I began reading a book entitled <u>Living Simply</u>. Chris and I had talked about the 'rat race' of life. *Is there a message here,* I wondered? I mentioned it to Bishop Mark and he suggested that I pray about it. Bishop Matthews thinks I should ask someone on the COM what they meant by "formation"...that little word that gets thrown around to make one question who they are and what they're doing. Rural ministry...*what would that be like*, I wondered? It would be a family, quiet atmosphere to live in, nice for grandkids to visit. I went with a couple from St. Timothy's in Herndon on a little trip to West VA, to a pumpkin farm...there it was, rural West Virginia. It was peaceful, quiet...*would Chris like this...would I like this...could we really live like this?* I really needed to pray about it . . .

It was Wednesday, November 27, 1996. I attended a beautiful service at Christ Church, Alexandria. Bishop Mark was the preacher. His homily was on Thanksgiving and its origin as a national holiday: Abraham Lincoln at the time of the Civil War. Lincoln designated it a national holiday with these words in 1863:

> "It is the duty of nations as well as of men to owe their dependence upon the overruling power of God; to

confess their sins and transgressions in humble sorrow, yet with assured hope that genuine repentance will lead to mercy and pardon; and to recognize the sublime truth, that those nations are blessed whose God is the Lord."

Bishop Mark added wouldn't he love to hear a political leader today acknowledge God as the Lord! The rest of his sermon was forceful, powerful, full of passion. I remember feeling the power of his words, and when he spoke before the offertory sentence about historical revisionists "making me sick," I felt a warmth for his integrity. Then when he said, "Ascribe to the Lord the honor due his name. . ." I was reduced to tears. *People should indeed do that*, I thought, *but they don't!*

In a meeting with Bishop Mark, we talked about what I feel I needed to do: focus on my inner being, reading spiritual giants, for instance. I began transcribing one of his courses about the "greats" in the church... Augustine, Gregory the Great, and others. I found their stories comforting and similar in the area of disappointment! I felt so connected to their stories. The detachment from the world creates a longing for God which in turn makes us see the *need* for God all around, the inadequacies of the world, the poor, the needy, the helpless. When I thought about others in this way, their needs before my own, it helped me see the bigger picture, which, on a good day, helped me feel less defeated. *There has to be light at the end of the tunnel... doesn't there?*

It was a Sunday morning in early December. I was back home and very distracted. I wasn't really prepared for the worship service. I didn't have the hymn books and service music prepared. It took longer than it should have to go from the entrance hymn to the Trisagion. Everything felt awkward. It was two weeks before Christmas. Half of Advent was gone. *What have I done to prepare for that holy day?* Not much, I'm afraid. I've been so caught up with moving Lisa and Ian in with us, so much anxiety over Jason. Lots of frustration. Sometimes I feel like I just don't care. I have a job. I'm the organist and choir director at St. Peter's in Narragansett. I have so much still to do to prepare for the Christmas music. But I'm totally unmotivated.

As I was driving home I found myself thinking about the "greats" in the church, about Gregory and Anselm, their dis-attachment...as they put it. There was such a void in my heart, an ache in my soul, the pain of being in a holding pattern. "A broken spirit and a contrite heart you will not despise; you desire truth in the inward part, a broken spirit and a contrite heart." A portion of a psalm and another set of lyrics from one of my cassettes! The words brought tears. I do sometimes feel that I have a broken spirit. Chris said last night jokingly that "romance sucked." He was smiling but I know he meant it. I've been a lousy wife. I'm tired, I don't care, surely feeling sorry for myself. The needs are so great. We search for what? For God, of course, but most people don't know it. They fill up life with things, money, stuff . . . when all they need is God. I drove by the Baptist Church. The sign read: "The void in your life can only be filled by God." I just ached; maybe I don't even know why.

As I poured through old journals and go back to a time when my life was in such disarray, I found a letter I had written to Paul Coyne. Paul and my daughter Lisa were separated and Lisa and son Ian were living with us on Cliff Avenue. I could see the writing on the wall; Paul's behavior at this time in his son's life would have lasting consequences and I needed to tell him so. It was shortly after Christmas in 1996. My former father-in-law, Lisa's grandfather, was dying. I wrote the following to Paul:

Dear Paul,

I visited the Roberts yesterday. Grandpa Roberts is dying. You may not have known that. He had chemo some time ago on a tumor in his chest. The doctors felt it was arrested. Apparently after a recent hospital stay, the tumor has doubled and I guess it's just a matter of time. I wasn't told that; it's obvious to the casual observer, but no one voices reality. Perhaps if they did, family members would be able to say how they really feel, express their fears and concerns, talk about the past, and plans for the future. But, they can't do that. They don't usually talk much to each other, especially about their feelings.

Mike was there, too, with his family. I watched him looking at his father, helping him to the bathroom, helping him into bed. This six-foot tall, strong man, now bent over, gaunt and needing to be helped into bed at 7:30pm on Christmas Day.

Some time later as I was leaving, I found Mike sitting on the outside front step having a cigarette. I knew he was doing more than sitting there smoking. I sat down beside him and put my arm around him. "It's hard to watch him like that, isn't it," I said.

"Yeah," he said, and began to weep. "I've tried to be so much like him all my life," he said, wiping his eyes. You're right, I thought. Your father smoked his whole life, and so do you. He's got lung cancer; you're well on your way. Most of his life he was unexpressive of his feelings, tried to be tough— so are you. You've pretty much succeeded in your quest, I thought, but a miracle has happened. You're looking at the man you've emulated your whole life, he's dying, and you don't want that to happen to you—at least not that way. So here you are thinking about the past, unable to deal with the future, and incapable of voicing the present because it hurts too much... Those were my thoughts, but they were certainly inappropriate to voice. All I could do was put my arm around him and comfort him.

"At a time like this it's really important to say how you feel—Dad too—so they'll be no regrets when he's gone," I said. "He won't be here next Christmas," Mike said, wiping his eyes. "I know," I said, "That's why it's important to get in touch with reality and your feelings." We sat quietly for a few moments.

He turned toward me and said, "I'm sorry for what I did to you."

"I know," I said. "Thanks for saying that." We both allowed as how we were young and unprepared for marriage but we wouldn't change anything of our lives today. "You can't change the past," I said, "Perhaps the sadness is not just about dad but about the fact that you are indeed like him. If that's not what you want, it's not too late to change. If you think he made mistakes with his kids, you don't want to do the same with your kids." That made him cry a little more. Actually, we both cried. A few more things were said—I can't remember what. I got up to leave.

"Thanks, kid," he said.

"Take care of yourself," I replied and I went home, a little shaken but thankful that he was not beyond some self-discovery.

I hope at this point you're beginning to understand why I'm telling you this. Mike is 17 years past the time when he stopped doing the right thing by his kids. Your time is just beginning and you have a choice to make: which is greater...your love for your son or your anger toward your wife? The answer should be the former, but your actions speak to the latter, and I believe Ian knows it. He is very bright, very sensitive. He hasn't seen pleasant conversation between you and his mother in at least 6 months, maybe more. What that says to Ian is: they care more about each other's anger than they do about loving me. I've been there and I know what I'm talking about. In this threesome, Lisa's feelings are not important...your feelings are not important...Ian's are. And the reality of the situation is unless you put yourself aside for your son and learn how to communicate with his mother, Ian will suffer and many years from now you will regret your actions and it will be too late to reverse Ian's scars.

The reality is your marriage is over; it never should have begun in the first place. You are both good people but you were mismatched. Out of that marriage, however, came something wonderful: your son and my grandson. Don't destroy the opportunity you have to make his life as normal as possible...

Elizabeth

As I read those words...words I wrote over twenty-five years ago, I am reminded of all the pain and hurt we cause each other when we forget our purpose in life. We're all good people, but we manage to make so many bad choices, don't we?

It's been quite a long time since I've worked on this manuscript: it's January 2020. I'm leaving the past behind for a few minutes and jumping ahead because it feels important. I just turned 72 and stepped into mandatory retirement. It's only been a couple of days and it's actually been eventless. But a little thing happened today that made me stop and actually get emotional. You'll hear more about the retirement event later, but today...this is about Ed Wagner. Who is Ed Wagner? Ed Wagner is one of about ten people who had received mailed copies of my sermons each week. He and his wife were winter parishioners for almost my entire time at St. Francis. A few years ago she died and he didn't return to St. Francis, but he wrote to me and said he wondered if I could mail him my sermons. So Ed Wagner became one of the few who received weekly sermons. I thought of Ed Wagner today...out of the blue...while I was telling Joel about putting a special note in my last sermon mailing. As I was telling Joel, I could barely get the words out without breaking down.

I quickly put my sun glasses on; we were in McDonald's...it was a Saturday noon treat! I wondered how Ed Wagner was going to be...not that *without* my sermons he would be devastated, but there would be another space to fill. I guess this is what it's going to be like for me, as I remember things that will be no more. It's a good thing that God's got all this.

Now, let's go back to our "regular scheduled programming." Where were we? Oh, yes, just before 1997...

Journal Entry: January 4, 1997. *I've already broken my New Year's resolution. Actually, I never really started it or verbalized it. Through December I kept saying when January came I'd get on my prayer schedule. It didn't happen. My whole life is a prayer, I thought, but I know that's a cop out. Am I afraid to be intimate with my God again? Have I been avoiding our relationship? Of course I have! I feel I've been let down. All those years, ups and downs...what happens now? If one doesn't care about a relationship, the relationship dies, or at the very least, it's terribly weakened. We were so close. The intimate language of Gregory and Anselm is so true, so accurate. Have I lost that? Or have You been here all the time? Why do I ask such foolish questions? Of course, You've been here, waiting, watching from that once cozy, inviting space which is now so cluttered with stuff. Help me simplify my mind again, or at least help me discipline myself to find that place in the morning, while the world is still asleep, where you and I can have our intimate moment, where we can get to know each other again. I miss You. Life has not been the same without You...*

As I read those words from my journal I remember all too well how painful that part of my life was. I was in such need of

101

resolution to so many things. I was glad I had the organist gig at St. Peter's, but being around the priest who had made my life a living hell wasn't easy. I knew there was more, but the questions were many: Where? When? How? The answers were about to come.

I remember the phone call like it was yesterday. Monday, February 3, 1997. A couple of weeks earlier I had contacted Lorne, asking for his help. He knew all the reasons I was given regarding ordination denial were simply because I was a conservative female and he was willing to go to bat for me with John Howe, Bishop of the Diocese of Central Florida. Chris was home sick that day so he listened in on the conversation:

"I've talked to the Bishop and the Canon to the Ordinary. And I have good news and bad news." That's a great way to start a conversation.

"Give me the good news first," I said.

"Well, Bishop Howe said that if my parish would support you, and if you were willing to go through some of the process again to fulfill the requirements in another diocese, he would do what he could to get you ordained." I held my breath for a moment.

"And what's the bad news?"

"You have to be down here in Florida on Saturday!"

I was speechless. Then the details and reasons began to emerge. The beginning of the ordination process starts with an event called a Conference on Ministry. Anyone who feels they have a call to ordination must attend such a conference. If the result of the conference makes one feel that they must pursue a call, the wheels begin to turn. The next conference would be in a few months, so this one—six days from now—was the better choice.

"Coming to this conference will push you along as quickly as possible. Sunday we'll meet with the Trinity Vestry to gather support. You won't have to move until the summer. We will back date your residency to the date of the conference: February 8, 1997. I've talked to the right people about your difficulty with testing. There are other ways to show proficiency...etc. etc."

This train was moving faster than I had ever dreamed. Summer? Moving? How can all this possibly happen? My silence and stuttering was broken by Chris. "She'll be there," he said.

Just the week before it had felt like all the cards were stacked against me moving forward: my supporting rector had left the diocese and taken a position in Florida, the one supporting priest on the Commission had died, and even the RI Bishop, who was willing to back me, even though I was conservative, had left the diocese! So, out of the blue, Florida became a possibility! Chris had once told me that the last place he'd ever want to live was Florida. Now, this… once again, God's timing is perfect.

Monday to Friday was somewhat of a blur…making plane reservations (I'd never flown alone)…renting a car (never did that alone either)…driving to a place I'd never been (and this was before cell phones and "talking" directions). I get lost in a paper bag; how was I going to pull this off? If God wanted these things to be successful, I had to trust him.

> *In God whose word I praise,*
> *in God I trust; I am not afraid;*
> *what can flesh do to me?*
> Psalm 56:4

Journal Entry, 6pm, Sunday, February 9, 1997. *I sit in the airport waiting for dinner. My flight leaves at 7:50pm. I don't know where to begin. The fact that I even did this on my own is a miracle in itself. I arrived at a little local motel in St. Cloud, Florida, on Friday about 6pm. It wasn't a bad room, but it turned out to be very noisy. The road was like West Main Road in Middletown at 5pm. I had a great chicken pot pie and mashed potatoes at Kentucky Fried Chicken…comfort food, I told myself. I didn't get much sleep—maybe because of the noise—maybe because of the excitement.*

I actually found my way to the conference where I met so many happy, joyful people. Everyone told their stories—one after the other each talked about the Spirit and Jesus in their lives and how they had come to this point. I was so overwhelmed that when it came to me, all I could say at the beginning was, "I am overwhelmed by the love and joy in this room…" And I began to cry! I told them where I was from, a place where this kind of talk wasn't readily acceptable, where trust in God's control is frowned

103

upon, at least in my experience. I said I'd graduated from seminary and had been dropped from the process. There were gasps all over the room. I apparently opened the floodgates because every other person who shared ended up in tears along with me. After lunch there was a presentation by a priest, a vocational deacon, and a lay person. Lay ministry is apparently a big thing in Central Florida.

At the end of the three presentations, one question was asked of the group. Focusing on the lay person's presentation, we were asked: "Would this person need to be ordained to be effective?" That's a powerful question. It offers much to think about if someone feels a call to ministry but is not sure about ordination. The rest of the time was spent in discussing the nuts and bolts of the process. Much didn't apply to my situation, but the following did. The Canon to the Ordinary said, "We are very flexible in this diocese. God has done the calling, not the Commission on Ministry. The COM feels it's their job to help to find out what God's call is." How refreshing! God had indeed called me, now I had to find out where and to what.

After the conference Canon Bennett and I talked for a while...My situation is different... Bishop Howe trusts and respects Lorne...would probably respond to Lorne's request... could set up a Bishop interview just before the April conference...Lorne should write the Bishop with his requests on Monday...Not to worry about residency requirement.... So much to think about...

It was a half-hour drive to Vero Beach after the meeting. Had a nice dinner with the Coyles. I filled in all the blanks from the past three years. It was a wonderful experience to be supported and cared for. It's been a long time...

Three Sunday morning services. So much to think about. I know I will have no peace if I do not follow God's Will. Be not afraid— the stamina will come—the money will come—all will be supplied if this is God's Will...

Journal Entry, March 22, 1997. *A little more than a month until our trip to Florida and I'm excited and anxious. So many thoughts and questions: How am I going to satisfy the qualifications? My mind races so much. I can't seem to focus as often as I'd like. And Bob Bergen's conversation with Russ! [Bob*

104

was a member of my Discernment Committee.] *Can you believe he would have gone to Russ, angry that the diocese had let me go and wanting to write to the bishop and Russ's response was that he didn't think I was that serious! What did he think I was doing for the past 13 years of my life?!!*

As I read my journal entries, so many years later, I'm amazed that my sanity prevailed. People supporting me...people against me...a lot of energy focused on me. Should I have been flattered, or is it sad that so much effort was expended on holding me down? I'm different...very different. Not the polished Anglican that is in the RI image.

Perhaps I will have to work harder to be accepted here and yet, that wouldn't be me, would it? I come alive on Sunday. I never thought that music would play as vital a role in my ministry as I now know it will. Terry Fullam keeps coming to mind. I will indeed use music—perhaps in sermons—who knows. Definitely in teaching. Music draws people together. It is a leveler, of sorts. And it certainly is a powerful method of praise. But that's the future. This is the present...

It was the summer of 1997. The word is determination. I remember sitting in my car at the McDonald's in Newport, eating my lunch and looking out the window in a daze. I didn't even look down when I reached for the French fries. I knew where they were. I've done it so often—just eating and gazing, enjoying a few quiet peaceful moments. A man got out of his truck and stuffed his empty bag into an already over-flowing trash can. He pushed and pushed until at least one small portion of the paper bag caught the plastic flap of the trash can, so his trash remained hanging, partly in, partly out. He had barely shut his door when a very large seagull swooped down followed by a smaller one. They surveyed the situation and the larger one went straight for the trash can. He wrapped his beak around the hanging bag, tugging and pulling until it fell to the ground. Even though it was closed tightly the bird began to shake the bag with a vengeance. Then he put it on the ground, held it down with his feet and peeled back the tightly closed paper with his beak. *Suppose, after all this work, the bag is empty,* I thought. What would the seagull do next? I didn't have to wait long to find out. The bag wasn't

105

empty. In very short order, the bag was open and the bird then proceeded to pick up the bag and shake it all around until the ground was littered with French fries. Finally—food! His determination and drive had won him the prize!

As I watched both seagulls eating the cold French fries, I thought of myself. *We are very much alike*, I thought. As I prepare to leave for Florida with its subsequent intern program and ordination next year, I think about the drive and determination that has brought me to this point in time, the things I've done over the past thirteen years—like that seagull, pulling and tugging at that bag in the trash can. And every hurdle along the way was a lot like shaking a tightly closed lunch bag, hoping to obtain a desired result, determined to continue until the goal had been reached. I thought of the many times I could have given up along the way because it was too difficult. But mere survival drove me on. Like that seagull fighting for sustenance, I too was fighting for my life, for my entire reason for existence. I watched as the gull and his companion devoured the scraps and off they flew. They'd succeeded in their task. They were satisfied. As I packed up my own trash, I thought about the larger scale of Christianity. Are we as determined as those seagulls to be fed? Do we fight any obstacle to gain the prize? Do we press on or do we give up at the first sign of difficulty? Being a Christian is hard work, but that's a story for another day.

CHAPTER 7

1044A Royal Palm Boulevard
Vero Beach, Florida

> A lovely place to call home...at least for now. Half of a duplex, outfitted for me, across the street from the church!

I sat in Bishop Howe's office in Orlando, Florida. It was September 29, 1997. Even though no one actually came out and said ordination would be a "done deal," it felt like God was beginning to open doors. Canon Bennett had said I'd already been through the most intensive part. So we stopped at the diocesan office as a courtesy on our way to Vero Beach. He also implied that "someone" could decide to accept me as a postulant which would mean cutting six months off my time here in Florida...and of course that 'someone' would be the Bishop.

At my first meeting with the PDC (Parish Discernment Committee) my COM advocate, while explaining to the group what their job was, said that the result of this process wasn't a rubber stamp. Then out of the other side of his mouth he said that when they made their recommendation to the COM it would be for Candidacy, meaning the bishop had ALREADY accepted me as a postulant! The group also decided at that meeting, after conferring with Lorne, that they would get a recommendation to him by Christmas! That will mean a vestry recommendation in January, three one-on-one meetings with three COM members who take their recommendation back to the entire COM. Then, God willing, I would become an official Candidate...*finally!*

Now, we get down to the "nuts and bolts" of where I was at that time. When Lorne said that his parish would take care of everything I would need, he wasn't kidding. Chris returned home and I was left in a duplex apartment across the street from the church, completely outfitted with everything from furniture to flatware. I had a place to live, rent free, owned by the church. I hadn't imagined things would be so perfect! I would be there for perhaps eight to nine months, so I would probably need a part-time job for spending money, or to at least feed myself.

In the meantime, Bishop Howe wanted me to have a mentor other than Lorne. His name was Pierre Whalon, rector of St. Andrew's, Ft. Pierce. By coincidence, his father was one of the two men doing rehabilitation on the organ at St. Peter's in Narragansett. I had met him a few months back! He was also a GOE (General Ordination Examination) creator and reader. What a small world, and that did make me very nervous. Perhaps he would want to read my GOEs and I wasn't excited about that, even though Lorne had said he didn't agree totally with the reader's comments. Anyway, we had a great visit, and he basically said that he was going to talk to the Bishop and tell him that "we've got a winner here." Boy, was that nice to hear! He also said that he had an idea for a part time job for me but he wanted to pass it by Lorne and the Bishop first.

On my way back to the apartment after that meeting, I thought, *Okay, God, now I may have two job offers. I don't want to make a choice. I expect you to eliminate one of them!* Earlier that week, Jane Coyle had suggested that I might work where she worked with Child and Family Services.

The next day I expected to hear about Jane's job. I didn't. That night I got a call from Pierre. The job offer was Interim Youth Pastor—2-3 hrs on Sunday nights, 2-3 hours on Wednesday nights, probably 4-5 hours preparation, with almost as much money as the other 20 hr. job!! So I took it! In the meantime, I sent my GOEs to Pierre and simply held my breath!

It was my first Sunday at St. Andrew's Church with the youth. WITH GOD ALL THINGS ARE POSSIBLE was the theme for the day. I was asked to tell my story to the middle school Sunday School class. It was energizing as I began from 1983 and told them all the impossible things that never should have been realized. It made me humble indeed, but it also excited me for the next chapter. *What do you have in store for me next, Lord?*

I went to the Youth Group that Sunday night just to observe. The format was really great. There was some type of worship and Bible study in the chapel. While that was going on, a parent was working on dinner for the group, i.e. pizza, Kentucky Fried Chicken, whatever they had signed up for. After dinner, a parent had a program assignment, some type of fun thing where they play a game that had a moral or promoted a value. It worked really well.

Wednesday night, however, was different. I was basically there supervising the kids while the adults were in their Bible study group. Kids were doing homework; some wanted to talk. It was great to have that time and space carved out to take a breath and get to know the kids.

One afternoon I went on a pastoral call with Fr. George. He was a part-time priest at Trinity, Vero, and did most of the visitations. Lorne thought I should go with him on some of his calls and learn how to "listen with God's ear." And my first visit was really a reality check—a far cry from the glory of liturgy. The couple was in their 40s. He'd been disabled for about nine years with a back injury. She was in an accident and last week had four vertebrae fused and was in one of those stiff collars. Fr. George and I were met at the door by the woman, a Doberman and a Rottweiler! I thought I was going to hyperventilate! On top of that, she was a heavy smoker and the house smelled awful. All that notwithstanding, after a lovely conversation we all had communion and Fr. George anointed them. The dogs stayed in the room the whole time, one of them nosing around me. As if that wasn't bad enough, the Rottweiler was lying on the floor with his butt facing me and he farted during a silent pause in the communion service! Boy, is THAT the real world or what?

That afternoon I saw Pierre. He'd read my GOEs and he said, "Let's go through some of the problems I saw in a couple of areas." So we did. I answered most of his questions and he said things like, "I knew you knew this" or "You were under pressure; that's why you didn't write that." etc. etc. etc. One time he asked me something I really didn't know and I got up tight—you know, change of posture, body language, etc. And he said, "Listen, relax. When we finish going through these, we're going to throw them away, never to be seen again. You ARE going to be ordained you know!" I almost fell off the chair! Actually I started to cry—BIG SURPRISE! He just smiled. So we finished the GOEs and spent the rest of the time talking about the youth program.

One of my problem areas in GOEs had to do with the Book of Revelation. I said that I knew very little about that book and that it intimidated me. Wrong thing to say! His response was, "Great. That will be your first Bible study with the Youth!" So the following Sunday, the kids and I began working on Revelation. God help me! I guess He's going to use whatever he gives me to do, along with the youth program, to help me over those things where I might be weak. All I can say is, God's got this...He *has* to!

Thursday was a lovely chapel service and Bible study, or B.S. as it shows up in the calendar. (Don't you think we should have a different abbreviation for that?) Thursday noon I went to lunch with a member of my committee. She took me to the yacht club where we went last April with the vestry. It was gorgeous, lunching in view of the pool!! Lorne had provided me with some funds to take each member of the PDC and Vestry to lunch for some one-on-one time. Friday I had another lunch at a *different* yacht club over a *different* pool with another member of the PDC. I'm supposed to be paying for these luncheons but I haven't yet been able to pick up the tab. The members wouldn't hear of it. Friday night was a pool party at the Pelican Club in Ft. Pierce with the Youth Group. It was nice to see the kids socially like that and to meet some more parents. We ate from a 7 ft. long sub sandwich, complete with chips and soda. It was right on a river between the intra-coastal waterway and Rt. 1. I think someone said we were on an island, but what do I know? I took pictures of the kids, a beautiful rainbow, and a pelican—of all things! And, I got tons of bug bites. At night down here they have loads of tiny little black bugs that you can barely see, and do they bite! I must have had an allergic reaction, too, because I woke up at 4am the next morning SO itchy that I had to go out to an all-night drug store for some Benadryl.

Saturday was the crowning glory of the week. From 9 to 3, I participated in Holy Spirit Day. This day is part of a larger program called Alpha, a 10-week experience created by Nicky Gumbel, a priest on staff at a church in London who studied law at Cambridge and theology at Oxford. The program deals with questions like: What is the purpose of life? What happens when we die? Why did Jesus have to die? What relevance does the Bible have for our lives today? Who is Jesus? Who is the Holy Spirit? etc. You get the point. Trinity offered this program twice a year, one night a week for 10 weeks, with a Holy Spirit day (all day Saturday) in the middle. Lorne has newcomers take this

110

course and, if anyone wants to marry here or have a child baptized here, they need to take this course sometime within a year.

> *"Remain in me,*
> *as I also remain in you.*
> *No branch can bear fruit by itself:*
> *it must remain in the vine.*
> John 15:4a

Anyway, today dealt with three talks: 1. Who is the Holy Spirit? 2. How can I be filled with the Spirit? and 3. How can I make the most of the rest of my life? Needless to say, it was a heavy day. After the second talk, we went into the chapel (about 30 people), had some WONDERFUL praise music. The young man who played the guitar and sang was as Spirit-filled as I've ever heard. He sounded like some of the tapes I have. Anyway, Fr. Bob, the assistant who facilitated the program, invited people to come forward for the laying on of hands, praying for the Holy Spirit. That's putting it in one sentence, but he explained beautifully the concept of the various manifestations of the Spirit. I ended up being part of one of the prayer teams—three women, Fr. Bob and another man. Bob said to the other man, "I want you to stand with Elizabeth in case someone she prays with falls back so you can catch him! We never know what's going to happen, so we have to be prepared. Just let them down gently so they don't hit their head." *Good grief,* I said to myself. I was simply hoping I'd have the words to pray with someone, let alone worry about whether or not they were going to fall and get a concussion! To make a long story short, which is difficult for me, I watched one man go down flat and I watched a woman tremble uncontrollably in my hands and then fall to the ground in 'holy laughter.' I'd only read about it, but then I saw it! Not weird, a little different, but tolerable. The day certainly gave me a lot to think about. And this program? It's worth my time and I'll certainly have it in MY church.

Three very profound things have come from the last couple of days. During one of the times of prayer at the Holy Spirit Day, I was touched to tears, and that very moment Fr. Bob began to talk about the fruit of the Spirit and how tears are from the Spirit. I recalled the invasive visit I'd had with RI Bishop Geralyn Wolf, when she questioned my tears. It was all clear now. When the Spirit moves in me, I often cry. It's that simple. Part of me wants to write to her and tell her, but... The second profound thing was in a sermon last Sunday. "It's not enough to be a believer. You must become a disciple. Disciples follow Jesus and that means doing as he did." Lorne said that believers simply show up on Sunday morning and then leave unchanged. Boy, is it good to hear sermons with substance and challenges! And the third thing? If you really know and believe Scripture, there is no gray—only black and white. I heard that and thought about how many times I'd been told that our Church IS the gray area! I'm doing my best to get re-indoctrinated again—to the truth.

The next few months were filled with so many challenges. There were PDC meetings, welcoming luncheons in my honor, and lots of time to observe how a church looks in the hands of committed Christians. One special Saturday night, I had a glimpse of what I was missing at home. Believe it or not, I got to babysit with some great kids—Christina, 9 (going on 30), Robby 7, and Anna Lee, 4. They were absolutely delightful. Christina was very helpful in the kitchen helping me get dinner. Robby was chastised by Anna Lee for starting to eat before we were all "sitting as a family." And Robby tried to get a second dessert out of me, to which the two girls replied, "Mommy wouldn't let you have it, so you can't have it!" Of was so much fun, reminding me of my most important vocation: being a mother and a grandmother. After dinner, while watching *Mrs. Doubtfire*, Anna Lee said to me, "Do you think you're a good babysitter?" to which I replied, "What do *you* think?" And she said, "Yes!" and jumped into my lap to watch the rest of the movie and she ended up falling asleep! It was such fun; it made me miss Ian and Erin terribly.

The next night Sunday was the first night of my St. Andrew's Youth Group assignment—alone! It probably went as well as could be expected, but I left there thinking it was a flop (at least my portion, anyway)! I was well prepared—as far as Revelation was concerned. My plan was to give them an overview—the who, what, and why of it. I felt that setting the stage was important before we got into the actual text. They needed to know what was going on at the time, what the atmosphere was for Christians, etc.

Well, the unexpected started fairly quickly—kids looking interested, kids looking glazed, at least one kid having all the answers and challenging me, particularly when I said that you couldn't take this book literally. Well, I managed to get through it all, but working with youth isn't an easy job. Actually I found it more intimidating than I expected. But I knew God would use it. If nothing else, I learned very quickly that I wanted to delve more into Scripture. Funny how that gets lost in seminary; grades overshadowed the learning, especially when you lack confidence in what God has prepared for you to accomplish. That is a difficult place to be.

There was one special evening that occurred during this time. It was as if God was putting his arm around me saying, *Relax...it's going to be okay*. It was a simple dinner invitation from Pierre and his wife Melinda, but it was the conversation that gave me the sense of God. I knew that Pierre was from Rhode Island, but I found out that he went to school at the Portsmouth Priory. I immediately thought of Fr. Christopher and asked if by chance Pierre knew him. "Of course I do," he said. "He was my theology teacher." It was 1969, only nine years after I had experience the holiness of Fr. Christopher myself at Holy Ghost Church in Tiverton. God brought me back to a place of comfort at a time when I so needed it.

There were hospital visits, prayer and praise groups and a few opportunities to take walks over the Barber Bridge. I lived close enough to drive to the parking area on the other side early in the morning and walk back and forth over the bridge. The intra-coastal waterway is so beautiful. One can forget anything and everything while gazing at God's creation. One morning I noticed some disturbance in the water below. As I stopped to look I saw about six dolphin playing, jumping over one another, one appearing to have something very much attached to her underside. It was quite small in size and salmon color. I don't know anything about dolphin babies, but perhaps it was a baby not to long after birth. It was really something to behold, watching all this sweet activity in the water below. It broke my walking stride, to say the least, but the same was true for at least a half a dozen other people! How could we not stop, observe and smile at the beauty of it all.

I have a faint memory of Thursday Bible studies after the 9am Holy Eucharist. I'd only experienced Bible studies with four or five persons in attendance, and here was a group of almost seventy people and we were studying the book of Leviticus! *Really?* I was blown away that so many people would be interested in that book of the Bible. It seemed ironic in a church where we focus on the love of God to be studying the book of laws! Yet, if God devoted seven entire chapters to atonement for sin, it must mean that it has a place in the church today. If we believe that the Bible is alive and relevant today, why aren't more Christians interested in God's teaching on sin? I came in part way through the study because it had been going on for several months, but what I heard was a blessing. It made me look at the depth to which we should live our lives in the service of our God.

I recall two nights around this time that brought my small world together, examples of two poles, opposite yet connected. I had lunch at the home of a member of my PDC and her home was to die for...large glass doors everywhere, five bathrooms, a huge kitchen and eating area that overlooked a small pool with an attached Jacuzzi and waterfall. The living room overlooked a babbling river. And there was an entirely separate guest area, outdoor grill, bar and refrigerator. It was almost too much, especially when the next night I was thrust back into the real world with a group of youth and their needs. It was the Saturday night of a Happening weekend. I was asked to join the other clergy that particular night to help with young people who might want to talk. The kids ranged in age from 10th graders to freshman in college, and I had the privilege of talking to four kids that night. What I heard will remain in my heart forever. High school, at the very least, should be a time of discovery and excitement. Instead there was so much pain—mothers who had run off and left children behind, abusive situations, fathers with guns. And what answers did I have? Just like Peter said to the lame man at the temple gate, "I give you what I have. . ." I couldn't change any of their horrific situations, but I could tell them to pray and trust God. Such faith under those circumstances I don't think I've ever seen in adults. I marveled at the trust these kids had to divulge their hurts and situations to a total stranger. How many more hurting people are there in the world that I might be able to touch, to turn in a different direction? I still wonder that today. The list will never be small, but God will always make Himself known if his children are willing to search for Him.

On this particular Wednesday in December, the walls finally came crashing down around me. Sure I've been learning lots of things, meeting people, working toward a goal, but the reality is this isn't easy. More and more I'd been thinking that I would never get through all this, that I wouldn't be what I needed to be. Was God really leading me to ordination? Pierre and I had a meeting scheduled, and he was late. It was the same day he would have to leave early to go to his daughter's soccer game, and I knew it. I was beginning to feel dismissed. I started listing all those times when I felt pushed aside—no one person that I felt truly free enough to share my soul with. *Everyone is too busy*, I thought. There *isn't* anyone; *I'm under a microscope with everyone, and no one to talk it out with.*

When Pierre arrived I was on the edge. He said, "So how are you doing?" As he unlocked his office door and we walked in, I said, "Oh, okay—I don't know—stressed, I guess." Then he said, "I was wondering when this was all going to get to you." And that was it! My eyes filled with tears and I lost it. I told him about the last PDC meeting and how I'd hoped to have heard something, but instead everything was going by the book and I'd know in another week. Before I said any more he said, "You're under a microscope; you *should* feel harassed; how long have you been doing this? Thirteen years? You *should* be pretty frustrated! Your family is 1500 miles away; you're tap-dancing for everyone. No wonder you're stressed!" At that moment, I had nothing left. I gave it all up. I told him I knew he too had my future in his hands, that I trusted him when he said that I *would be ordained,* but the stress had finally gotten to me. He said if he was supposed to recommend me for a PhD program, he would say no. But he would definitely recommend me as a parish priest, that there was no question in his mind that I had a call to ordination.

Over the next two hours, as I rode with Pierre to pick up his dog at the kennel, he shared his journey with me, a journey fraught with horror stories of being in churches with predecessor problems, being called to a parish where there had been embezzling going on, and many years of long, angry conversations with God. Pierre asked me if I might be angry with God for all that he had allowed to happen to me. I said I thought I'd dealt with it all, but maybe I hadn't. God surely knew at that moment how much I needed my 'safe place.' The final thing Pierre said that day was this: "With all that you've been through in the last few years, God must have something special planned for you!" And, by the way, since God knew all this would take place on that day, there was no soccer game.

Today was December 3, 1997. If I was made a Candidate by January, I could be ordained a transitional deacon in July 1998... My peace, however, was short-lived. I was told that a few on the PDC wanted me to preach at the 5pm service on Saturday, December 13th. It was not what I wanted to hear, not that I wouldn't like to preach but that it was on the idea of a command performance. I was told that a couple of committee members wanted to know just what I felt called to, that I couldn't do as a lay person! That's the question that I had grown to hate. I had been asked that years earlier and hearing it again at this point was upsetting. "Work your passion into your sermon," Lorne used to say. Then I *really* felt like I would be performing. *Lord, do I really have to perform to become what you want me to be?*

I was on my last nerve. I sat down and poured out my heart on paper:

Lorne,

We have never had any secrets; you know me pretty well and I think it's important that you know exactly where I am. I'm actually in a pretty lousy state at the moment. It's a little better today than Wednesday, but I'm still working through some things. You know, I've realized in the last few days just how alone I am at this point. It's not quite as alone as I was when I had no support in RI, but I'm nevertheless alone. I have to be "on" with everybody; everyone that I deal with is a potential vote. There's no one to whom I can confidentially share, cry, bitch, or even rejoice. You don't have the emotional energy right now to function as a spiritual director and in this process, it wouldn't be appropriate anyway. So that leaves me sitting on lots of stuff. I am prepared to be "on" as a priest for the rest of my life, but right now, I'm not a priest. I'm someone who is and has been under a microscope for years—someone who could have the rug pulled out from under her yet again, and the microscope has finally caught up with me.

God knew my need and he sent someone to me Wednesday afternoon when I least expected it. Hopefully, that "angel" will continue to be the person in my safe place.

116

Thursday morning — I missed Holy Eucharist and most of your class because I simply forgot, which I still can't believe! I was doing a lot of thinking and listening to some Psalms on audio tape and I forgot what day it was. I wasn't happy that I'd missed Eucharist or the class but I realized God was doing something else. The psalmist David and I have a lot in common. David knew that God was always with him and he would triumph in the end, but it's interesting that so many of his psalms are laments, cries of anguish, or down right anger at God. And that's where I am. When I talked to you Thursday afternoon, I knew that I needed to tell you all this. Asking me to preach on the 13th did it. Can I do it? Of course I can. I'm a good preacher. I'll do it joyfully, and I will preach the best sermon based on Scripture that I can! And about the specific that the PDC wants? I want to baptize people. I want to absolve people. I want to marry people. I want to bury people. I have a passion for preaching the Word of God. I want to work with families, helping them teach their children to know and love the Lord. To me, that means I'm called to be a parish priest! What else can I say? I don't know how God will stretch me in a parish. That remains to be seen. Some of that may or may not work into the sermon, but I'll do my best. I read the readings last night: 3 Advent, Rejoice Sunday (Gaudete Sunday)—wonderful, joyful OT and NT reading with John along side yelling "You brood of vipers! Who warned you..." Could be interesting...

Thanks for your time. I just wanted you to know where I am. Please keep me in your prayers as you are in mine.

In His love,
Elizabeth

It was a Thursday in December. I was getting close to the end of all the meetings and preparations and I could only wait for a final vote of confidence...a typical Thursday in the life of Trinity Church, Vero Beach. I attended a prayer meeting with the DOK (Daughters of the King) before the service and Bible study. As all different people and situations were being offered in prayer, I found myself praying for Jason. I do that every day anyway, but this time it was out loud in the presence of the group. The sisters were all there and echoed my prayer. Funny how one never stops being a mom, even with all that was going on in my life. But that's the way it's supposed to be. The comment that once your children turn 18 and move on...is crazy. It doesn't matter where life takes them, they are always on your mind and in your heart...for better or worse!

The morning service was especially powerful. I was a chalicist and I participated in the healing service. Such grace, but I couldn't get Jason out of my mind. After the Bible study we hurried over to the church to get a seat for the St. Edward's School Christmas Concert. It was so festive and made me long for Christmas back home with my family. And of course every tall, blonde young man that was in the group made me think of Jason. By the time all the beautiful music was done I was pretty much a basket case. I ended up in the assistant's office, talking about Jason and crying. He had once talked about his daughter who had been on drugs and was so messed up that he and his wife had put her out when she was 18. She was apparently okay now at 21, but he understood the pain I felt—the wounds that never heal.

About 1:30pm I came back to my apartment and I was totally exhausted, not exactly how I wanted to feel as I waited for the Parish Discernment Committee's vote tonight: 5pm. I made up my mind that I wasn't going to sit around waiting for the phone to ring, so I went to a friend's house for dinner.

This was a very complicated time for me. I had made some special friends in Vero Beach. It was a fun time, but that was coming to an end...one way or the other! I had become close to several of them and so I invited a number of the Boutique ladies over for tea and cinnamon sour dough. These were the ladies that had done such a beautiful job supplying me with everything I could possibly have needed during my stay in the apartment. I wanted them to see all that they had done for me and it was a fun time. People had been so caring and generous. Even though I hadn't yet heard from the committee, I still felt blessed.

Two days later—December 20, 1997—the vote was in: Yes! It was almost a let down in a way. It wasn't that I had come to the end of a long road; it was actually the beginning of an even more complicated one. But if I had gotten this far, God must have a plan.

Yes, God did have a plan, but there was still a little "muck" to deal with. Even though the PDC had voted yes, the Vestry had to also

118

agree and I learned that there were two people on the Vestry who had concerns, one in particular regarding something I couldn't fix: I'm a woman! I was beginning to feel like Job. *Really, God? How much more??*

Å positive vote did go through, but there was one little sadness in it. Typically the Sr. Warden is a presenter at an ordination ceremony and the Sr. Warden said he couldn't do it because I was a woman. A suggestion was offered that he might plan to be out of town on that day—whatever day it would be. It's kind of sad, but I guess such a plan allows everybody to be true to their convictions. There are some days when I actually wonder if I've lost my mind to go through all this when experiencing potholes all along the way. God must indeed be in control, because if I stopped and thought about all this too long, I might have thrown in the towel!

The year 1998 was a year that would be full of frustration, joy, sadness...whatever emotion you like, it was there. After the holidays, being back in seminary was stress-filled, listening to my friends talk about their June or July ordination dates, what positions they might be getting...and me? I was just hoping to finish out the semester with some idea of what was waiting for me.

It was April and I was tasked to write a report for the Vestry of Trinity Vero. It's kind of ironic that the title of my report was supposed to be "Where have I been and where am I going?" God has a sense of humor, indeed!

Where have I been and where am I going? April 1998

Six months have passed since I began my internship here in Florida. This program consists of responsibilities at Trinity, Vero Beach and St. Andrew's, Ft. Pierce. At Trinity I am a Eucharistic Minister, attend mid-week Eucharist services and Bible studies, have preached three sermons, attended monthly ministry meetings, taught Communion classes, done hospital visitation one day a week. I attend staff meetings and have bi-monthly supervision meetings with the rector. I have also spent time with the ECW and the DOK learning how these wonderful ministries enhance a parish. At the beginning of this intern program I spent three months working with a Parish Discernment Committee, meeting regularly for the purpose of discerning my call.

Besides my work here at Trinity, a portion of each week is spent at St. Andrew's, Ft. Pierce. I have weekly meetings with Fr. Pierre Whalon who was appointed by Bishop Howe as my mentor. I am also working there as a part-time Interim Youth Minister.

In December Trinity's vote to support me for postulancy was sent to the diocese and the Commission on Ministry followed up with the next step which was to call for the required psychological and psychiatric testing. I had done similar testing previously in the Diocese of RI; however, the COM in Central Florida asked that I repeat the tests since new requirements have been added.

There are six required screenings:
1. A Life History Questionnaire
2. A Behavior Screening Questionnaire
3. MMPI-2
4. Incomplete sentences form
5. Spiritual gifts
6. Myers/Briggs

The Life History Questionnaire is a 23-page extensive questionnaire dealing with the following areas: family/social/developmental history, relationship and marital history; educational, occupational, medical, psychiatric, legal, and financial history.

The Behavior Screening Questionnaire asks questions dealing with such things as disciplinary actions, terminated employment, civil suits, and sexual ethics.

The MMPI-2 is an evaluation made up of approximately 575 statements to which the response is either true or false.

The Incomplete Sentences Form is 40 lines with one or two words per line with the instruction: Complete the sentence. For example: "Tomorrow _____." or "I love _____."

120

The Spiritual Gifts evaluation presents 100 statements dealing with 20 different spiritual gifts. The numerical answers (0 - 5), added up in a particular order, determine one's strongest spiritual gifts.

The Myers/Briggs evaluation determines one's personality type.

These evaluations were completed on March 30th at the Episcopal Counseling Center in Orlando. Discussion on these evaluations will take place on April 22nd with Dr. James Fisher, Ed.D, PY, LMFT. My husband Christian and I are scheduled for a psychiatric evaluation in Winter Park with a Dr. Joseph Muller. Within the next week the results of all written evaluations along with reports from Dr. Fisher and Dr. Muller will be sent to Canon Ernest Bennett in the Diocesan Offices. These reports are turned over to the COM who then makes a recommendation to the Standing Committee. I will then be asked to meet with the Standing Committee.

Let's see now. In the spring of 1998, all the final examinations and meetings took place. It was unnerving to be so close to the end and yet, not knowing for sure what the end will look like. Well, I know you peeked ahead and you know how this chapter ends. Yes, I was approved, made a candidate in June 1998 and an ordination date of January 16, 1999 was scheduled. But it wasn't without lots of stress and worry.

Toward the beginning of the summer, while I was still working at St. Andrews and doing things at Trinity, Vero, I remember many doubts: *How much more can I go through, Lord? Have I gone through all this for nothing?* Apparently the answer to the first question was: Much more will happen...the road forward still has a few twists and turns left...

Farewell party from Trinity, Vero 1998

My last Sunday at Trinity, Vero, was a lovely tribute to my nine months among those lovely people. It was indeed bitter sweet, however; many were so supportive but the "woman" issue was difficult to overlook. The only thing I had to go on was I believed that God had put me on this path and it was my job to follow. And follow I did!

CHAPTER 8

40 Division Street
Newport, Rhode Island

> A home on the historical register – Chris' parents' home…a second-floor apartment. A temporary arrangement until God showed us the plan…

Moving back home was strange. It wasn't really home. It was the second floor of Jack and Ruth Myers' home in Newport. Christopher and Diane had bought the house on Cliff Ave. and since our next home would be determined by the church that called me, this second floor life style would work if only temporary.

In my first draft of this manuscript I had the timeline wrong. Funny how your mind wants to forget certain times in your life. To the best of my recollection, Chris moved into this apartment late summer, early fall of 1998. I only remember coming home from my time in Vero Beach and doing a "job search" while sitting at the table in that second floor apartment.

My memory is a little vague but that would mean that I was there for only a couple of months before I went off to seminary. You know, as I think about it now, I'm in the dark how it all happened. Lots of assumptions were made…that I would be ordained…that we would be moving *somewhere*. I don't even recall discussions about all this; it simply happened.

So what do I remember about this particular "address"? Antiques, crooked floors, a feeling of being in a place where I didn't belong…actually it was a limbo of sorts…a stopping point, or a jumping off point, until I made it to the next step. Thanks to my son who helped my timeline, Chris and Diane moved into Cliff Avenue in October of 1998, the same month I interviewed at St. Francis. But I'm getting ahead of myself…

I began the job search and it was very discouraging. As I said early on, a conservative female in the Northeast would have limited options for church employment. *Lord, there've been a lot of ups and downs here. I'm ready for closure. What about you?*

CHAPTER 9

140 Loquat Road NE
Lake Placid, Florida

> My dream house in the middle of one and a half lots, situated on a canal, three bedrooms, an office, a big kitchen, a sitting room, a living room with a fireplace, overlooking the swimming pool, a two-car garage, big lanai. What more could I want?

The summer of 1998 was to be a new beginning. I was back home, sort of, and I was on my own with a job search. The Bishop had always said that he would do all he could to get me through the process, but he couldn't promise me a job. It would be up to me...and God, of course. So while I had an ordination date of January 16, 1999 on the calendar, I had no job prospects yet. Thinking about it now, it's actually amazing that I would press forward like I did...*me*...a person who typically holds back, doesn't defend herself, certainly doesn't take chances...and here I was sending out resumes in New England and actually a couple in Florida...not sure why...but the churches seemed promising. I guess even then I knew I was following God's lead, albeit without acknowledging it.

There was one funny story regarding an interview I had with the Deployment Officer in the Diocese of Connecticut. Chris and I sat in her office and after reading my application, she apparently realized I was conservative, and she said, "Well, there might be one or two churches that would be interested in you." The conversation went down hill from there, and she ended the interview by inviting us to lunch before we returned to Rhode Island.

She took us to this quaint little restaurant that was attached to a book store. The waiter was very pleasant, and actually cute, and I said as much to our host. She said, "Oh, he is more interested in your *husband* than in you!" When lunch was over, we exited the building through the book store which was overrun with erotic and distasteful pictures and books. You couldn't avoid looking at them. That was our last trip to the Diocese of Connecticut.

I don't remember Chris and I talking much about where I should look next. Thinking about it now, it was a little odd that we weren't sharing our thoughts about such a drastic move in both our lives. I don't know whether he actually thought I'd find something close to home, whether it didn't matter, or whether he thought I never *would* find a church that would be my calling. We never talked about it. Sounds odd, I know. His mother never really thought I'd make it. What was important to her was that I had a college education. In her mind, without that, a person wouldn't make it. So I kept sending out my resume and hoping God was guiding my choices.

Then came the answer. I received a call from Bishop Howe. He asked me how my job search was going. "Not very well," I said. "In that case, let me read you this church profile." And he proceeded to read me the church profile for St. Francis of Assisi Church in Lake Placid, Florida. It sounded like a lovely little church, and of course I asked if they were looking for an assistant, to which Bishop Howe replied, "No, they're looking for a rector!" I almost dropped the phone. "But I'm not even ordained a transitional deacon yet." One has to be a transitional deacon for six months before being ordained a priest, so this phone call didn't make sense to me. "You could be deacon-in-charge for six months," the Bishop said, "then you would be ordained a priest and become the rector." "I couldn't do that," I said. I may have a college degree and a masters in divinity under my belt, by I was still the same insecure person I'd always been. And his response? "Of course you can!" I repeated my doubtful response and he repeated his...again! Finally, I said, "Would you be a phone call away?" "Of course I would," he said. And that's how it all began.

He sent my resume to the Search Committee at St. Francis and they called me to set up a phone interview. I remember sitting in the upstairs room at my in-law's house on a conference call with a room full of people that I had never met. When the interview was over, they asked if we could come to Florida to meet them. I couldn't celebrate because I wasn't ordained, so we set up an Evening Prayer service on the Saturday evening of Columbus Day weekend, 1998.

I designed a service, complete with a bulletin of prayer, a sermon and music (of course, I played the piano...I wanted them to see *all*

125

my talents). After the service we had a lovely evening of food and fellowship at the home of the Sr. Warden. I was expecting a lot of questions because there were so many people there...the Search Committee and the Vestry, and their spouses. But the "third degree" never happened. It was an absolutely delightful evening, but as it drew to a close, I finally said, "Doesn't anyone have *anything* they want to ask me?" They looked at each other and finally one man said, "Would you wear your clergy collar?" *What an odd question!* I thought. I did find out some time later, however, that the priest that was at St. Francis before me hardly ever wore his collar. Few people in the community even knew he was a priest, which obviously annoyed the members of St. Francis. My response? I remember it well: "Listen, it's taken me thirteen years to get here. I'll probably sleep in that sucker!" Such a response didn't demonstrate much class, but they all laughed. There was one more question, directed to Chris. "What will you do here in Lake Placid?" they asked. Lake Placid is a quiet, little town in the middle of Florida, and there would be little opportunity for employment here in Chris' field of expertise. He wasn't yet at retirement age, so it was an appropriate question. His answer shocked me. He said, "I could get a job bagging groceries at Publix!" A strange answer, even a little funny, and all who heard it smiled and were satisfied. As I think about it now, we never even talked about his response afterwards. Perhaps we both knew that it would never happen...

The next morning was Sunday and we got to worship in St. Francis' beautiful little church. I don't remember if anyone there knew I had interviewed with their Search Committee the day before, but I do remember the afternoon festivities. They were dedicating their new parish hall and the priest who did the dedication was their former rector who had left six months earlier. The parish hall was standing room only and looked too small before they even got to use it, but that's all they could afford to build. Some time later I was told that the small addition, the kitchen, three bathrooms and a hallway from the church into the parish hall came at a cost of about $10,000! Amazing! A far cry from what was to come a few years down the road...

We left the next morning and drove to Orlando. I suggested that we stop in the diocesan office to see the Bishop before we left. We were ushered into the Bishop's office and he invited his Canon to the Ordinary Ernie Bennett to join us. We exchanged pleasantries and the Bishop casually said, "How soon can you move down here? I just received a call from the Sr. Warden at St. Francis and they are offering you the position!" Thinking about it now, I wonder what my face looked like! I'm sure my jaw dropped. Chris smiled as if he knew it was coming. "Well," I said, "I'd like to spend one more Christmas at home with my family." Remember it was Columbus Day weekend. "No, that's too far away," he said. "How soon can you be ordained?" That question was directed to both myself and Canon Bennett. According to the Canons of the Church, one must be a candidate for at least six months before being ordained a transitional deacon. I thought for a moment. "I think it would be around December 1st," I said. The Bishop directed his next question to Canon Bennett. "Are you able to supply at St. Francis for the month of November?" Canon Bennett checked his calendar and said that he was scheduled to serve at two other churches during that month. "Change them," said the Bishop, "I want you at St Francis for the month of November, preparing them for Elizabeth." And turning to me, he said, "Can you be here the second Sunday of November, and to be ordained on December 1st?" I'm sure I stuttered. Things were moving so fast. Chris and I looked at each other and we both said, "Sure," with no thought of how this was all going to happen. There was a phone call to Lorne, after the Bishop asked if I would want Lorne to preach. Lorne said absolutely and the plans were formalized.

> ...*Let nothing move you.*
> *Always give yourselves fully*
> *to the work of the Lord,*
> *because you know that your labor in the Lord*
> *is not in vain.*
> 1 Cor. 15:58

I have little recollection of the next four weeks. I was about to have a life-changing experience, as if what I had already been through wasn't enough! In less than four weeks, I would be moving to Lake Placid, Florida. I had no idea where I was going to live. I didn't know how long it would be before Chris retired. I was almost fifty years old and I was uprooting the life I knew, but starting *another* life I knew I was meant to have. Funny, as I think about it now, I just moved on ahead. Little planning, not much conversation, everything was just "matter of fact." I know it sounds crazy, but I guess that's how it works when your trust in God is pretty high. He had brought me this far. I'd just have to wait for the next details to surface.

At this point you may be wondering why I have said "I" so many times...why I haven't used the word "we." Truthfully, it's because Chris said very little. He was supportive of everything that was happening. Yet, we never even talked about how long he would work, when he would retire, where I would live...all the important things that we *should have* talked about. I'm not sure why that was. I can only think that I was afraid if I asked about all these important things, that something bad would happen and what few plans we had would go up in smoke. I do remember when he told his mother that he was planning to retire early, she was appalled. "You *can't* retire early!" she said. "Your daddy worked into his 70s. Besides, a man is defined by his vocation. You *can't* retire." That was the one and only thing Chris' mother ever said that was the gospel truth. But it would be a few years before either of us realized it.

The third Sunday of November was my first Sunday at St. Francis. Canon Bennett had had two weeks to prepare the congregation for my arrival, and on that Sunday, I preached. I guess it went well because they didn't ask me to leave. That weekend we looked for a house, and found the most beautiful place I'd ever seen...it was a dream house, in the middle of two lots with a swimming pool on a canal, six miles from the church. I stayed with a parishioner for a short time and when the purchase of the house was final, a moving van arrived with all our furniture. It was early December.

I remember it was a strange time...setting up a home where I would live alone for about a year and a half...getting used to life in a new part of the country...making new friends...learning new things. But being away from my children and grandchildren was the hardest. Chris came to visit as often as he could, but something was happening to me. I was developing a new sense of self, a trust in my decision-making. It wasn't a pulling away from Chris, but it was a moment in time where I began to feel that I had something to say, that my voice was important. People were looking to *me* for advice. This was a whole new ballgame. I began to think about things I had never been a part of, like paying bills, making household decisions. Oh, I'm not complaining; things just happened around me and I never paid much attention. Perhaps it's because I was never asked for my opinion. It was just like when I was a child. Everything was provided; I hardly had to ask for anything. I guess I was never allowed to grow up and take responsibility for myself. Yet, in other ways, I grew up fast because I was alone a lot. Oh, well, what did it matter how I got here. I was where God had placed me and I had to learn to live on my own for a short time.

As each day went by and I had a church full of people who looked up to me, I began to realize that I *did* have wisdom to offer, that I *did* have knowledge others viewed as helpful. It was a whole new me, and it was freeing and frightening as the same time. I wondered how this was all going to play out when Chris retired and moved to Florida.

**Diaconate Ordination
December 1, 1998**

I planned the transitional diaconate service complete with Ian, four years old and Erin, two years old, bringing up the elements. It was a beautiful service, most of which I remember from looking at photographs. Some of my children and grandchildren were there; it was truly a special night. There was even a busload of people from Trinity Church, Vero Beach, where I had done my intern work! And, believe it or not, the bus got lost on the way, and the service was held up for about twenty-five minutes! Late service notwithstanding, it was a glorious service.

It would be a year before Chris would be retiring and moving to Florida. While I took each day with great joy, doing what I believed I was meant to do, there were two defining moments in that year and a half that made me realize my happy home might be in jeopardy.

129

The first was a phone call from Jason. It wasn't so much that he was calling me from jail or that the conversation wasn't pleasant. The defining moment had to do with my response to his call. When a wife is incredibly upset about a phone call, you would think the next call would be to her husband. In this case, it wasn't; I called my Bishop. I remember it like it vividly. It was about 8:30 in the evening and the late hour never entered my mind. Bishop Howe had just experienced a traumatic event himself with his son and I guess I felt he would understand my state of mind. And actually, he did. He was so supportive and helped me tremendously. Why didn't I call Chris? I don't know. Maybe I thought he wouldn't understand how I felt. I don't even remember if I ever told him about the call. Guess it isn't important now...

The second defining moment for me was a silly conversation with Chris about our dining room table. We had received it along with a matching hutch from Chris' grandmother. She died just before we were married. She was a very sweet lady. Chris apparently had had a conversation with Meredith who was living in Las Vegas at that time. She happened to mention that she was looking for a round dining room table. "I told Meredith that she could have ours," Chris said to me on the phone one night. I lost it! For the first time in our twenty-plus years together I lost it! I cried and I yelled into the phone, "You gave that table away without talking to me first? You can't do that! Our family spent Christmases and birthdays and holidays around that table! It's the only remembrance I have left of home and my family! You can't take that away from me!" Chris was silent, and the subject of the dining room table was never mentioned again. Where did he put his feelings? Did he even have any to store? I never knew. I surprised myself with my reaction, but I guess it was the beginning of the rift. I think that's when we started to grow apart. We talked about nothing...but if you don't talk about things, they'll go away...or at least things won't change...right?

Chris came to Lake Placid as often as his job would allow. He attended St. Francis and made a few friends. By the time he retired and came to Florida permanently, his financial expertise was known to many and he was asked to chair the Finance Committee. I expressed concern as being the Rector's husband wasn't a good precedence, but the committee was adamant. In a small parish, expertise isn't readily available, so you have to take what's given to you. Chris became the chair of the finance committee and another rift began to emerge.

I was ordained priest on June 13, 1999. As I write this, I find that both ordinations have run together in my mind, that the confusion and upheaval I was having caused my memories to fade in a day-to-day attempt to manage each issue. Sad. But it was indeed a glorious day. I remember when all the attending priests laid hands on me. I was told that even though they would be "gentle", it felt like the weight of the world was being placed upon me, which I'm sure is exactly what it's meant to feel like.

It took only about three years for the wheels to come off the bus completely. And those years were awful. Sometimes I wondered where God was, how things could have deteriorated the way they did. I was so entrenched with the parish that I didn't notice the increase in Chris' drinking. What's to notice? He always had a martini or two after dinner…or maybe before…it wasn't until I started noticing his behavior and putting things together that I realized there was a problem. We often had gatherings at our home which included the parish, and often he'd had too much to drink. He became loud, a little off color, and even talking about things that I had told him in confidence. There were many awkward moments.

And there were those times when the kids came to visit. The interaction was uncomfortable. Specific incidents aren't important for this writing; my purpose here isn't to place a blame on anyone, but to look at me and my life at that point…and it was slowly going down hill.

I began getting up very early and going to work before Chris even got out of bed. I'd come home late as often as I could because it was to sad and painful to watch him get from the chair in the living room and stumble to the kitchen for another drink. One time I checked the Booth's gin bottle a few days in a row: 1.75 liter every other day was his consumption. What was I going to do? His mother's words rang in my ears day after day: *A man is defined by his vocation.* And of course, that was it in spades. Chris had no hobbies. He did a few things in the yard, but basically he spent his days staring at his computer screen. He did join the local Rotary Club and took on the secretary position. He spent all week making the minutes perfect. But that was about it. He took the Finance Committee very seriously, but there were those times when a decision fell to me, and he didn't like that.

I remember the time I had to leave a Finance Committee meeting for some reason, and when I got home that evening, he was in the kitchen waiting for me. He turned and, raising his voice, he said, "Don't you *ever* leave one of my meetings again!" I said nothing. I don't think I was afraid. The mood in the house was simply apathy, which is worse than yelling and screaming. A relationship void of feeling is doomed to failure. His mother was right. In his mind, he had no purpose. We shared very little. I couldn't trust telling him things that couldn't be repeated. So there was little to nothing between us.

When a young couple with children get divorced, you spend a lot of time trying to protect them from all the bad things that are happening, only to learn years later that your children knew everything that was going on around them anyway. That's exactly the way it was with the parish. While I thought they didn't notice anything, they saw the destruction unfolding before their eyes...every little comment, lack of contact...everything! And where was God in all this? I'm not sure I knew. Obviously he was present but I don't recall seeking him out...personally...very much. I lived for Sunday mornings. That was my life and I was afraid if I sought a divorce, I would lose my church and my position as rector.

I made some phone calls to find out if there was a divorce policy in the diocese. I learned there was no specific policy, that the Bishop took each situation on a "case-by-case" basis. Thank God for that! Some bishops make the priest leave so parishioners wouldn't find themselves having to take sides, especially if the spouse remains in the parish. I don't remember how or when we started talking divorce. Maybe it was after I purchased a new bedroom set and moved out of the bedroom into the extra bedroom. I remember that when the bedroom set was delivered, Chris said nothing. He did nothing. It was very strange. I do remember thinking that this was the first piece of furniture I had purchased in over twenty years, something that was mine. For our entire married life, our entire house was outfitted with his mother's furniture...old, antiques. Another area in our lives where there was no discussion. Thinking about it now, I can't believe I was like that. He just assumed that I would want this furniture, and I never balked. It was as if his mother could turn me into an acceptable, southern belle if I was around her furniture. Sounds nuts, but perhaps that's what she thought. I guess I should have been grateful, but by the time my new bedroom set arrived, I began to realize that I never liked what I had lived with for so many years...

Did you know that you can download on a computer all the paperwork you need to get a divorce? That's exactly what I did. Obviously it can only work if the divorce is amicable, and it was...sort of. The house was sold and it was just a matter of time before I found a place and Chris would move back to Rhode Island. I remember the day we went to the courthouse in Sebring. We were led into a room with a large conference table. The judge sat at one end and we sat across from each other. The judge looked at the paperwork, asked us if everything was the way we wanted it. We agreed, and he signed and stamped the divorce papers. "I wish *all* divorces were like this," he said. We shook hands, and that was it. Fifteen minutes erased about twenty-three years. Apathy...relief...I don't really remember. It surely was a load lifted.

CHAPTER 10
321 Belle Tower Avenue
Lake Placid, Florida

> Déjà vu... A mobile home a half mile from the church. Two bedrooms, two bathrooms, a nice kitchen, a large living room, a screened-in porch, a car port and a shed.

Tropical Harbor was the name of a mobile home park a few minutes from the church and I found myself a nice little place. It was partially furnished, so I didn't need much from Loquat Road. I didn't want much, just the bedroom set I had purchased. That was mine, and I did want his grandmother's dining room table and hutch. She liked me. They were a connection to my children, to better times, to Rhode Island, to days that were happy...

It was 2005 and I was alone again. I was making a new start. It was somewhat like seminary, but this time I had a parish family depending on me and supporting me. And I had to rebuild my relationship with God that I think was a little shallow. I always preached that the kind of Christian you are will show up most in what you do Monday through Saturday. While I was doing God's "work", what was I doing for my spiritual health? I had to look at that very closely.

It's strange that my way back to a stronger relationship with God came by way of my multiple photograph albums. How could that be? Let me explain. I had thirteen 12 x 12 albums filled with family photos—forty-plus years of pictures. One night I brought all the albums into the living room and put them on the floor beside the couch. I found five small boxes and placed them side by side on the coffee table. Each box had a name... Christian... Lisa... Meredith... Christopher... Jason. I *always* listed them chronologically. They are *all* my children. Nothing would take that away. I began to realize that growing meant a form of moving on, and for me, it meant giving to my children some of my memories. Book by book, I removed every photograph. Photo by photo, they went into a specific box. Of course, I kept a few, but I gave most of them away. I remember thinking, *what if they won't cherish them as I have?* I quickly realized that hat would be up to them. All I wanted to do was share my joy and I hoped that they would find joy in them as well. This might not sound like a big

134

deal, but I think it was as if I was letting my children go…again…letting them grow a little more into whom they were meant to be, perhaps in the next stage of their lives. Maybe it wouldn't mean anything to them, but it was something that I had to do. Each picture brought emotion to my heart, memories of all those years. It was a sad and happy time. It took me a week or so, but I will always remember that room, those moments I relived so many years that God gave me with all of them…my five children. I was alone and while some days it was lonely, most days were filled with relief. I had lovely neighbors. I was close to church, and the parish was very supportive. The nights were difficult. If I waited too long to go to bed, I seemed to get a second wind and I couldn't fall asleep. There was a television in the bedroom and I used to watch a DVD of *The Eagles in Concert*. My favorite song was *Love will keep us alive*. Kind of ironic, isn't it? If I was really tired, the song would make me cry. I wanted to believe that God had someone out there for me. I had to believe that I wouldn't be alone the rest of my life. That was my strongest prayer…I wanted to share my life with someone who would want the same things I wanted, someone to support me in my vocation, someone who truly loved God and trusted in his plan for us.

For the next few years I dove into the parish. We did a feasibility study with regard to another addition and with God's help and a lot of money—$350,000—, we more than doubled the parish hall and the kitchen and added a rector's office, an administrator's office, a youth room, a choir room and a library. And it only took eleven years to pay it all off! We were blessed. The parish grew in those years and I grew in confidence. I managed to visit my children a couple of times a year, but my home had truly become Lake Placid. *Where was that special person, Lord? How will I find him?*

Early in 2010 I got the bright idea to look into internet dating. Giving that I'm such an incurable romantic, I thought it was going to be an easy task: I would find someone and he would sweep me off my feet and we would live happily ever after. Some of my parishioners were even praying for "Prince Charming on his white horse." Well, not only did this process have bumps along the way, but there were potholes deep enough to swallow up the state of Rhode Island!

I'd open a profile, and if the photograph appealed to me, I'd read the profile. If I didn't feel a visual connection, I didn't bother pursuing it. I know that seems shallow, but perhaps God gives us those senses for a reason. Having said that, however, the visual is what got me into trouble almost every time.

There was one terribly handsome man with a great profile who responded so well to who I am. Through instant messaging he sounded romantic and pleasing and I began to get swept away. Then there were the red flags that I ignored. Whenever I would ask a personal question, he became very vague. He said his business took him out of the country. He would have to leave our conversations rather abruptly, and at one point he used the "God" card masterfully. He said, "Do you think God can forgive anything?" He knew that would get my attention and I immediately went into "priest-mode." He said he was mixed up with people from Saudi Arabia, something to do with oil—can't remember it all—but he wanted to get out of the business because it was dangerous and deceitful. He was seeking my help. I was a little slow to really grasp the insanity of all this, that while his words were seeking forgiveness from God, God was the farthest thing from his mind. He was trying to get into my head and use me to his advantage by asking me to "invest" in helping him get out of his difficult situation. I don't actually remember how it all ended except he stopped writing, telling me that he had gone to the authorities and they said they needed proof of all this before they could prosecute and he was leaving the country to obtain the proof. Yes, I know what your thinking... *she really is blonde , isn't she?* I did talk to a priest friend of mine and he managed to convince me, ever so gently, that the guy wasn't who he said he was.

There were many e-mails after that, the majority unanswered. But what did I expect? The first line alone of my profile would certainly scare away most guys: "A gentleman in my parish told me that I'm a crazy lady into which God poured a priest...and that is what I am." That would be a deal-breaker for most men. But I couldn't deny who and what I am. God would have to take care of the rest.

I was on "Match.com," "Plenty of Fish", "Love and Seek," "eVow," "SeniorPeopleMeet.com", and "eHarmony." In the beginning it was kind of fun to come home at night and look at

136

some of the responses as well as those that were initiated from the guys themselves. I learned quickly that I'm at a funny age for searching. Younger men were typically *too* young. It felt like I was dating a son and their capacity for conversation and comfortability was very limited. But men my age and a little older *looked* and *acted* old or they were looking for a traveling companion. Many of them simply wanted to go fishing, boating, or just sit around, watching the neighbors go by! That would have made me crazy!!

And then there were the ones that really were just crazy, like the 35 year-old, black guy with dreadlocks who said I was gorgeous and he wanted to meet me, or the 85 year-old man right in Lake Placid who wanted me to meet him at an antique auction. (He told me exactly where he would be sitting and that I only needed to come by and check him out, and I didn't even have to make myself known).

Now when I read a profile I liked, I'd say that I liked the picture and the profile and I'd add something like... *So if you read my profile and my vocation doesn't intimidate you, you know how to find me...* I kept track of the "no response" messages. I stopped counting at 126, and that was after profiling over 10,000 men! Not a very good percentage of response. My experiences ranged from the painful to the bizarre.

Albert was my most painful experience and it taught me the most important lesson. He turned out to be a scammer. The red flags were there, but I wanted a relationship so badly, I simply ignored them. Not wanting to be alone is a very powerful urge. I ended up losing a large sum of money before I discovered that he was part of a celebrated group on a web site called "Romance Scammers." He was possibly from Nigeria, using the photos of some other very handsome man and he played on all the vulnerabilities in my profile and my comments. A very painful lesson indeed, but I became very good at recognizing scammers after that.

I remember that I had told my children about Albert when I had visited. I must have looked and sounded like a school girl because at least one of the kids laughed. When it all fell apart, I wrote the following e-mail to them, and a received some sweet responses:

August 7, 2010

Dear children,

   Just wanted to let you all know that you were right to be skeptical.... it was all a scam.... Two of my friends "googled" Albert and found a Scam page. Check it out, if you like.... Albert Papadopolous, Tampa....

   Seems that a couple of other women have posted their experiences. He's used "Rick" as another name... also Christopher Anderson. Practically his entire profile is there....

   My friends stopped by to tell me. Ironically, at that very moment I happened to be on IM Yahoo with Albert, or whatever his name is. I asked him if the name Christopher Anderson rang a bell. Can't remember what he said, but I responded with, "You're very good at what you do, Albert. Thank you for a special couple of weeks, even if it wasn't real. But shame on you for pulling the "God" card. I don't know what you've done with other ladies, but you pulled in a very big fish with me. Shame on me for being so honest and open...

   So there we are, guys. I'm not sure how I feel... I'm a little numb... I feel very foolish.... It's funny... a couple of lines from tomorrow's sermon are: Store up for yourselves treasures that won't wear out.... be prepared for the enemy is always lurking....

   Ironic isn't it? The next time.... if there is a next...I won't drag you all into it....even though it brought smiles to all of you... especially since you saw something that hasn't been there in a long time...

   I'll be ok. There are people here who watch out for me....

All my love,
Mom

While I think I heard from all my kids, I did get written responses from three of them:

   Well, he's an a?@# ! And you are in no way foolish. I say you're brave and beautiful for putting yourself out there & I would venture to guess that Albert is not the norm.
   Love you!
   Meredith

I was actually considering googling him myself, but then thought better of it. And I'm glad it wasn't me who found it (and I just googled it myself to confirm). I really am sorry, Mom. I'm a skeptic by nature, and you are not, and your vulnerable trusting nature was taken advantage of.

That is just wrong. I'm just glad it didn't drag on for you. Time will heal, though scars remain. And don't be afraid to "drag us in" if there is a "next time". We can still be voices of encouragement as well as voices of reason when you need it.

Christopher

Hey ma, Sorry to hear what that a$&% did to you! Don't worry, the trick that I do is don't look for love, it will find you.

Love you

Jason

Wow! Truer words were never spoken, but I'd have to wait a little longer to be found...

Then there was John from Lakeland who seemed on the surface to be rather funny. When he suggested that we meet somewhere in between, I suggested WalMart. Then we'd look for a restaurant from there. Since the meeting day was a Saturday he said that he hadn't planned on going out that day (he wanted to stay home and watch football—and *that* should have been a BIG red flag for me)—but then he added, "Why don't I get a hotel room in Lakeland. We can watch the football game and then make our own "half time show." When I said that he was apparently on a different page than me, he said, "Well, I thought that since we lived so far apart we might want to get "that part" out of the way, and if that worked, then we could decide if we *liked* each other!" True story! And I thought *I* was insecure! Now, *there* was a man who thought so little of *himself!* Needless to say, we never did meet.

And then there was Bill, a.k.a George McFly... or at least that's who he reminded me of. He seemed nice enough on the phone, but a man who has a picture taken in a suit and tie, leaning on a fluffy white rug should have been a sign of strange things to come. We met at Woody's Barbeque in Lake Wales. He looked shorter and heavier than his picture. His hair was slicked back. He had on a brand new pair of jeans, pulled up *way* too high—they even looked hard like they had just come off the rack—brand new white sneakers—even a shirt with a pocket-protector! Now you see why I called him George McFly?! And the conversation was just as bizarre. Right off the bat he said that his son hoped he'd meet a woman who could straighten him out! As if that wasn't crazy enough, he looked at me and said, "You have nice skin." A very strange pick-up line. At another point during lunch, he said, "You have nice hair." He even asked me if I had blue contacts because my eyes were too blue to be real! I couldn't finish my lunch and get out of there fast enough! Poor man—he even called me later to ask what he had done wrong so he could change. I actually told him that I didn't feel comfortable answering that question because I was sure there was someone out there for him... just the way he was...and he'd just have to keep looking...

Well, at that point, I considered stopping this insanity. I wasn't going to find anyone on the internet. I tried altering my profile... adding another photo or two, changing a few words. And then Ralph came along. When talking to others about him, he became known as "The Dancer." He lived right here in Lake Placid. We met for coffee and hit it off right away. He was delightful and he said that he liked me. *That's a start*, I thought. He was about ready for retirement and was considering all the things on his bucket list, one of which was learning ballroom dancing. So he asked if I'd like to come over to his house on Sunday afternoon. He had some dancing lessons on tape. He'd been teaching himself and was ready for a partner. That afternoon we danced for almost three hours. We ended up sitting on the love seat together and he kissed me, and it was obvious that he wanted more. One thing led to another and I realized that I couldn't respond to what he wanted to do. I said that I wouldn't be able to look at myself in mirror in the morning if I let all this happen, and I must say he was very kind. He said all the right words, like he wouldn't want to hurt me and that the time had to be right. I thought about it all week, wondering what it would be like to have that feeling again. *I do like him*, I said to myself, and I was sure that he cared for me. (In retrospect, "I care about you" seemed to be the mantra of his relationship with me. Those words seemed to satisfy the moment while allowing no commitment...) Writing about "The Dancer", however, made me realize that I almost reverted back to my insecure self.

140

There were two dances after that at the Moose Lodge. They were really fun, but the connection   was definitely distant. We sat at a table and I'm not sure we talked...just waited for a song. It was strange. And then came the Josh Turner Concert, November 4th, 2010, at the college in Avon Park. I had purchased two tickets several months earlier in the hopes that I would have a date. So I asked Ralph and he said he'd go with me. That night I was dressed to the nines and he looked sharp in his suit and tie. It was actually funny to watch all the people gathering for the concert. I had forgotten what part of the country I was in along with the fact that Josh Turner is "country." Lots of the guys that attended the concert showed up in cowboy attire and boots! I didn't care; I felt special. It'd been a long time since I'd been anywhere dressed up. Funny though, when Ralph picked me up, he never said a word about the way I looked. I was disappointed.

The Concert, however, was wonderful as Josh went back and forth between his various song styles. Ralph didn't seem to respond one way or the other, even though on the way home he did say that the concert of wonderful. But the realization that any kind of connection with him was never to be, came toward the end of the concert. During one of Josh's love songs the word "alone" appeared in my mind and almost literally before my eyes. It was very clear, and I knew exactly what it meant. Ralph and I were sitting side by side that night, but I was alone. And I finally felt it.

Toward the end of the concert, while I was thinking about this revelation of being alone, Turner announced his last song . He said that he hoped it would bring peace. As the song began it sounded like an old spiritual. It was called "Jesus is the Answer." He spoke of a "Man" you could count on, someone who would always be there for you...a Lover...an Understander. And before I knew it, the one thousand-plus concert goers erupted into applause, a standing ovation with arms in the air! Ralph remained seated. I was in tears and I knew that the words were meant for me...and the song continued... Of course, Jesus is the Answer, the Anchor, everything I needed.

We left the concert together...but I was still alone. We made small talk on the drive home. He said that he enjoyed it, but I found myself thinking I had gotten all dressed up that night *for myself*; certainly it wasn't for someone who didn't notice.

A week went by and, by the grace of God, I was able to *not* call him. Oh, yes, he would have been amenable to another dance date and maybe even another after hours event, but I came to the painful realization that he was getting what he wanted... and I wasn't, at least not totally. I was thinking one night about the one red flag that I had chosen to ignore: he had casually mentioned wanting both of us to continue on our internet search, because we needed to find the "perfect" match. That certainly sounded like one who isn't committed. He didn't have to be, when there would always be another woman handy to fill the bill at any moment.

As the days went by and I accepted that without my initiation, there would be no relationship, I had a talk with God: "Father, I get it ! Ralph isn't the one and Jesus is the answer. But I need more, so you need to find someone for me! You need to send someone, and not sometime in the future. It needs to be now!" That's sort of the long and the short of it. And I remember weeping and falling asleep...

As I approach the end of my story—
with only one more address to go—
the truth is that it's really
the beginning of my story.

It's the story that I prayed for all my life.
It's the story of two very different individuals,
brought together by circumstances
that could only have been orchestrated by God.

It's a story of love and romance
that every little girl dreams of
and *mine* came true...

This amazing story begins the very week after the concert with Ralph. I'd made up my mind that I was *done* with looking for the right person to spend my life with. Oh, I still dreamed of finding someone, but this particular way wasn't working for me. So how was I going to find just the *right* person? I had no idea. But I thought... *Go ahead, look at your e-mail...just one more time.* And there he was...the one God had chosen for me from the beginning, and it wouldn't take very long before we both knew it.

Match.com had sent me what *they* said was a "match." This was the teaser...53, looking for a woman between 44 and 54, within 50 miles of Lehigh Acres! Were they crazy? Why did they send this profile to me? I was over 60 and, not knowing where Lehigh Acres was, meant it wasn't close by. But I read the profile anyway. There were things that were in no way a match; yet, there were words and phrases that spoke volumes. Here's the profile I was sent:

yeahsureitis23
Old Skool New Skool Guy
- 53-year-old man
- Lehigh Acres, Florida, United States
- seeking women 44-54
- within 50 miles of Lehigh Acres, Florida, United States
- Relationships: Divorced

- Have kids: Yes, and they live away from home (3)
- Want kids: Probably not
- Ethnicity: White / Caucasian
- Body type: About average
- Height: 5'8" (173cms)
- Religion: Christian / Other
- Smoke: No Way

- Drink: Moderately

Hi! You are looking at the profile of one unique and interesting guy! I am a very active and fun loving guy, as well as a dedicated father and business owner. I love music and concerts, walking or hiking, riding bicycle, cooking, motorcycles, hot rods, deep sea fishing, snorkeling or working on my home. I have quality tastes and search out the new and unusual. I have a great sense of humor and am a nice person!

I am searching for a like spirit, someone intelligent and fun loving, but has values and ideals. A free spirit, someone I crave to spend my time with. You must like the outdoors, at least some of the time, like to travel and entertain, have and appreciate ethics and character. Be good at conversation and have an interest in the world. Let's discover it together!

My job: I do commercial tree work and love being up close and personal with plants and animals in spite of the difficulty and risk. My work is also seasonal, time off in the winter and spring. My job is also my prime exercise!

My religion: I have a very strong faith, but seem to not fit into organized Churches.

Favorite things: I am very into music, Blues and alternative rock mostly, but I like a lot of other genres too. I like movies rather than TV, a wide variety, but stuff from the Cohen brothers are my favorites.

Last read:
I love to read and have all my life, but time seems a little shorter now. I read when I can.
I was floored! So many things jumped out at me... *I am a dedicated father and business owner... I seek a like spirit, someone intelligent... someone with values and ideals... someone I crave to spend time with... someone who appreciates ethics and character... be good at conversation..."* No matter what the differences, I knew I had to respond. But I had been disappointed so many times before. Could this really be possible? I prayed, sighed deeply, and e-mailed him back, knowing that my profile *did not* appear when he had signed on that morning. One more chance...just maybe...oh, I so hoped he would respond. I pressed SEND.

144

Hi,

   The system sent you to me as a "match" but there are some things that don't match. You seek someone younger, and I'm farther away than you seek, but nothing ventured nothing gained. If I interest you and you're not intimidated by my vocation, you know how to find me. Elizabeth

I don't know if *I* would have responded to that e-mail. The e-mail did sound as if I didn't care if he responded. For a fleeting moment, maybe I didn't. I was so tired of being hurt, of being taken for a fool. But guess what happened? He responded to my e-mail! His name was Joel. I learned much later that he had been attracted to my vocation. He had served on a church committee that screened persons who were interested in ministry. He told me that two of the three persons he worked with were women. And he understood what it meant to have a "call." Not only that, but he had been attracted to the traits that went along with the call to ministry. Only God could have put all those pieces together...for sure! I had finally found a man of God.

We e-mailed back and forth for almost a week. He told me that he had been divorced for eight years and that he had raised two of his three daughters alone, which was his greatest accomplishment in life. It didn't take long before the e-mails turned to phone calls and then we met.

It was Sunday, November 14, 2010. About 12:30pm that day, I was in my office hanging up my vestment, getting ready to head home, and the phone rang. "I can't wait any longer to meet you," he said. Such precious words, someone who felt so connected to me already that he *needed* to meet me. "Meet me at the park just over the LaBelle Bridge." Now I didn't usually venture out on my own, to meet a stranger in a strange park. But I somehow knew that it would be okay. The feelings inside me were just crazy. I hurried home and I changed my outfit three times before I left the house! I know we were just going to be sitting in a park, but I only had one chance to make the right impression.

Driving time was about fifty minutes. I had indicated earlier that I typically get lost in a paper bag, so he suggested that we talk as I came closer to the destination. Even doing that, I missed the turn and drove right by the park! After turning around and circling back, I pulled into the park. He got out of his truck, I got out of my car and we got that first glance. Actually, I think I saw him first, his back to me as he exited his truck. I remember thinking: *I changed three times and he's in a black t-shirt, jeans, and black sneakers?* I'm such a snob! But that line of thinking disappeared fast when he turned around. What a wonderful smile! "Hi, I'm Joel," he said. And the afternoon began.

The Labelle Bridge reminded me of a similar bridge on Cape Cod. It separated a quaint little town with little shops where everybody knew everybody. There was a sloping hill between our parked vehicles and the water, and he suggested that we sit for a bit and talk. What a breath of fresh air: a man who wanted to talk! We talked about children, jobs, likes, dislikes. It was amazingly comfortable. *Take your time*, I thought. *Go slow with your feelings...*

Then Joel suggested we take a walk under the bridge and down an historic part of LaBelle. There were beautiful old trees all around, breaking up the sidewalks, making the walk such that you needed to be careful. And this beautiful man that I had just met...took my hand. That did it! I don't think I'd ever held like that before...strong, weathered, a working man's hand...*like Peter*, I thought. As we walked through this quiet, little town, he asked me the question *no other date* had ever asked. He wanted to know all about my journey to the priesthood. I didn't even know this man and I already felt validated, that someone finally cared enough about who I *really* was inside,

Asking someone who has been through such a convoluted journey to the priesthood was like opening Pandora's Box. I began to tell my story, and before I realized it, at least an hour had passed and we were still walking. I began to wonder if we would be able to find our way back since we had walked so far away from where we started. Joel said, "You keep talking; I know where we are and I'll get us back." Truer words were never spoken—I knew I had finally found someone special. When we had begun the walk we happened upon a beautiful, old tree growing out of the sidewalk. It was magnificent. Joel told me how the sidewalk had been replaced many times as the roots grew bigger and broke the sidewalk that was there. As we looked at the tree together and he marveled at its beauty, it was plain to see his profession: he's was an arborist, a lover of God's trees. He said that his mother had

146

wanted him to go to college, but his choice, his fulfillment was working with his hands.

We were together in the park and the surrounding area for over three hours. It was amazing that so much time had gone by! Dinner wasn't part of the plan, but it was getting late. "Can you stay longer and we'll look for a place to eat?" he said. "Absolutely," I said. *Are you kidding? Of course I need more time with this man!* Not much is open on Sundays, but there was a little place he called a "redneck" bar. Not exactly a classy choice for a first date, but it didn't matter to me at all. It was a spur-of-the-moment thing. He even joked about it, and said what I had been thinking. I didn't think there was anything else to talk about, but our conversation and connection continued. He even held my hands across the table. It seems funny to feel like a teenager at 62 years old! But it felt so real, so precious...

While waiting for our dinner to come, I found myself thinking about "grace." Should I say grace...will it be too much...how will he react? Before I came up with an answer, our dinner came and *Joel* said, "Would you bless the food?" *Who is this man and where has he been all my life,* I thought. I was embarrassed by my thoughts. How could I have wondered if saying grace would bother him. Once again I realized that I had indeed been led to a man of God.

After dinner Joel took me back to my car at the park under the LaBelle Bridge, and we talked on the phone most of my way home. So much to process, to revisit. Luckily the ride isn't long and without traffic, it's rather pleasant. The next morning I was greeted with a phone call. As if that wasn't enough, he followed up with an e-mail:

Monday, November 15, 2010, 6:49am
Subject: Monday morning

OK, Elizabeth, I know we just talked on the phone (it was a nice way to wake up!) and I plan to call you while on my way to work, but I like to write too so will leave a few lines in your mailbox! I don't have to tell you what a joy it is to know you and how much I have enjoyed your company and conversation so far, but I certainly want too! I would have never guessed that someone like you was around the corner from me and you have already

147

*enriched my life in ways I am still thinking about. God has truly
given me a gift in providing me with your friendship! I am also
now way behind in the gift department over what I have received
from Him as opposed to what I have done. A time to make
changes in my life is here. I also wanted to thank you for blessing
our food yesterday, that has always been my job at home and it
was nice for you to do it for us. You WILL hear me pray, though
most of my prayers are done when I am alone. A good weeks'
wishes and I will be hearing your sweet voice in only a few
minutes!   Love, Joel*

Four days had passed since Joel and I met at the park and we were
about to have our second date—a *real* dinner date. Could I let
myself believe this is what I had prayed for...what friends of mine
had prayed for? I should have been scared to death. I should have
feared that I was being taken for a ride once more. I'd been down
this path before. But I had an unexplainable peace about this
relationship and what seemed to be developing. It made little
sense that I would feel this way after such a short time, but all I
could think of was God was in the mix. Our conversations and
phone calls and e-mails were sweet and kind and God was part of
them all. *So...could it be...?*

Thursday, November 18th. It was a lovely little restaurant at the
end of the LaBelle Bridge...Forrey's Grill. I got there first, and
I'm almost embarrassed to say that I had brought a candle with
me. It had to be just right. The table was next to the window and
I sat facing the door...watching...waiting. I felt like a school girl.
Did anybody around me notice? Then Joel walked in. We smiled
at each other, said 'hi' and the memories began. It was funny
watching the wait staff. They smiled at us, catching a glimpse of
what was going on every time they walked by. Flashing across
my mind was a line from "The Lion King" when Timon sees
Simba and Nala "rubbing noses" and Timon says, "Ah, a budding
romance in the savannah..." We weren't male and female lion
cubs, but it surely looked like 'a budding romance.' My memory
of the conversation is minimal...back to our past and my call. But
what I *do* remember is it felt right. That's all I can say. And I felt
safe, cared for, respected, protected. Thinking about it now, it's
amazing that face-to-face conversation can bring so much life and
joy.

Of course the dinner was over too soon, and Joel asked if I'd like to go into the bar and sit for a bit, perhaps have a drink. This time we sat on the same side of the booth! I always wondered why couples did that; it always seemed awkward. Now I get it! Later Joel told me that he had all he could do to *not* kiss me right then. Wow...such honesty...where did *that* come from? He said he resisted the urge so as to not make a scene. Silly boy! "Never hesitate! I'm fine with PDAs!" I told him later.

It was getting late and I really had to leave, although I didn't *want* to. We'd had such a precious evening, one I'd never forget no matter what happened next. The parking lot was somewhat deserted since Joel had parked on the back side of the restaurant. He walked me to my car and... Well, the short version is this: 45 minutes later, we were still standing outside my car, "making out"! I don't think I'd ever done that before. The restaurant had closed. The bartender and the last waitress came out, and we were startled when they said, "Didn't you two leave a long time ago?" "Yep!" we answered back. The bartender said, "It feels like I'm in a high school parking lot," to which we said "Yep!" It was dark and they couldn't see that my face was red. It was as if someone was going to call my mother and I was going to get grounded. It was crazy, beautiful, silly, and wonderful on so many levels. Don't ever let anyone tell you that falling in love has an age limit. It doesn't.

A day or two later I was sitting in a restaurant in town with a friend. I don't remember what we were talking about, but an old song was playing over their sound system. I didn't know the artist, and I could hardly understand the words in the verses, but I did remember the chorus from so many years ago: *I knew I loved you before I met you, I think I dreamed you into life. I knew I loved you before I met you , I have been waiting all my life!* I was in the middle of a conversation with my friend and I actually stopped... in mid sentence... to listen. Those words...the message...I couldn't wait to get home to "google" the song lyrics. God works in mysterious ways. He gave me a song...He gave *us* a song...more than that...a calling. It was perfect.

Joel came to the Ecumenical Thanksgiving Service on Sunday, November 21st, at St. James Catholic Church in Lake Placid. He got to meet a couple of my friends as well as enjoy the service with some wonderful singing. While I was sitting on the altar with the other Lake Placid clergy, I would look out toward Row 5, where Joel was sitting, and would often find Joel looking at me. The church was full, but it was as if we were the only two there.

In the past five years holidays were a little difficult for me. Even though there were invitations from various parishioners, I still missed family. Thanksgiving was one of those holidays where we celebrated on the following weekend and finished the day by decorating the Christmas tree. Wonderful memories. But I sensed that this year would be special. Joel and I were planning to spend Thanksgiving together at my house. I was to have a minor surgical procedure the day before and I thought I should lay low. But our plans were changed, as often happens when you have children. Joel's youngest daughter was coming home from college to spend it with her dad. So "dad" said that he would like me to spend Thanksgiving with them, and if I wasn't up to driving, he would come for me. He surely had the "caring" and "protecting" stuff down pat! I did end up feeling well enough to drive myself and I felt amazingly comfortable in his kitchen, even though at that point, I wasn't sure about the adult children. I was remembering what it was like when I met Chris. All our children were much younger, less intimidating. Adult children are much different when it comes to their parent's relationships.
Joel was outside smoking the turkey and I was inside preparing the other things while I visited with two of his daughters. It was more comfortable than I had expected, but I couldn't help but think: *My children are twenty years older than these girls!* God does indeed have a sense of humor,

We had known each other less than three weeks and it was clear that something wonderful was happening. We talked and prayed together every morning and he still sent me a short e-mail around 6:44 EVERY MORNING. He called me at lunch. We talked and prayed together in the evening. We had dinner in LaBelle once during the week and he came up on weekends for church. Everything was happening so fast. It was frighteningly wonderful. It felt right. *He could be the one*, I thought. But the biggest hurdle was yet to come.

Christmas morning after the service, I flew north to visit my children, as I had done for many years. But this year I asked Joel if he would like to join me on the weekend to meet my children and my sisters. *What on earth was I thinking?* To tell you the truth, I don't really remember! I was just so excited for them to meet this wonderful man that had already changed my life. We had only known each other for five weeks! But it just felt right. I don't know how else to explain it. I had prayed for such a relationship, and now that it was likely here, I was frightened to death!

Pictures would have told this part of the story much better, but none are to be had. The looks on my children's faces when I told them about Joel...and that he was coming up to meet them! I felt like a school girl bringing my boyfriend home to meet my parents. In hindsight, though, I was blessed to have children who cared enough about my well-being to be skeptical. They'd been through this with me before, hearing about strange men and seeing their mother being taken for a fool. But I believed this was different, and I tried to tell them as much. Funny, that the only two who *really* got it at first were my two oldest grandchildren: Ian and Erin.

After about 24 hours with my children I realized how awkward this visit was going to be. Lisa wasn't too receptive to Joel spending two days in her house with me. Joel picked up on the difference in my voice when we spoke on the phone those couple of days after Christmas. I learned that Christian was still having a hard time with his dad and I being divorced, let alone meeting a new person in my life. So when Lisa asked me not to "talk so much" about Joel, I honored her request, albeit with a little sadness. I was so happy and I wanted to share it. All I could do was take my grandchildren Christmas shopping, enjoy their company, and hope that Joel's visit would show them what I already knew.

When Wednesday came that week Rob took the afternoon off to take me to the airport. He felt it was important that some member of the family was with me... "After all, what would he think if no one but mom went to the airport?" His offer to come with me turned out to be exactly the right move. When all three of us left the airport I suggested that Joel sit in the front so the "boys" could talk to each other. Well, in the short 40-minute drive to Lisa and Rob's house, one would have thought that Rob and Joel were separated at birth! They had multiple interests between them—

motorheads, hot sauce, guns, not to mention both had three daughters almost the same age. Even Rob and Joel's birthdays... only four days apart!

That night Rob, Lisa, Ian, Joel and I went out to dinner. When Joel left the table for a moment, Ian looked over at me and said, "I want to ask him one question: 'What are your intentions with my grandmother?'" We were all shocked, and I was highly impressed! It's pretty special to have a grandson who cared that much. Rob said that he shouldn't ask, but I told Ian he could ask Joel anything. He didn't ask...at least not that night.

The next morning Joel and I went to breakfast at Chris' and Diane's. I remember walking into the kitchen. It couldn't have been more awkward! First of all, I was walking into what was *my home* several years earlier, but the owners had changed. I introduced Joel, we exchanged a few words, and Chris continued cooking breakfast. Joel was wonderful to put himself through this. Later he said he was fine with the "moderate inquisition," but it was so strange, being on the opposite side of questions and concerns. Mostly it was comfortable, the six of us at the dining room table, Chris sitting in the spot where his father used to sit. Chris told me later that waiting for us to arrive that morning was probably akin to what it would be like "checking out" a suitor of daughter Erin. He mentioned a line from a country song that came to mind... "I'll probably be up all night cleaning my gun."

Joel and I weren't in the car but a moment or two when I received a text message. It was from Ian: "Gramma, Erin just texted me. She said Joel's OK!" I learned later that after our dinner the night before Ian had texted Erin with his approval, so now Erin had to report in!

The next "inquisition" was in Tiverton with my two sisters, and this was a classic. We went to Ella's apartment. It was somewhat amusing actually. She had two chairs set up, side by side, facing the couch where Joel and I were asked to sit. It would definitely be an inquisition! Joel handled himself fine, as I knew he would. Questions, answers, a few smiles. But he funniest thing happened when we were getting ready to leave. Joel thought he'd reassure them with, "You don't have to worry about Elizabeth. I know how to drive (referring to his motorcycle)," to which Maureen replied, "I don't *care* about you; I care about my sister!" Only

God knows why Joel didn't just bolt at that point. By the way, did I mention all the little old ladies at church who kept threatening Joel if he hurt me? Obviously, what he felt was real, or he surely would have headed for the hills.

The next night there was a gathering of all the children and grandchildren at Meredith's and Mike's house...upwards of fifteen family members. It started out a little awkward; he was the only stranger there. But Ian and Erin managed to gather the grandchildren in a separate room and we had a little visit with all of them. There was one wonderful moment during the evening that I'll always remember.

Their Christmas tradition was to get together at a sibling's home and have a "Secret Santa" event where they would exchange insignificant gifts, or steal someone's else's gift that had already been received. (I guess you have to be there!) There was a lot of chatter and laughter going on and even though I was with family, it was the kind of uncomfortable that happens when the 'visitor'— family or not—isn't around very much. There are jokes and comments that would need explanation, and both Joel and I were somewhat out of the loop. Well, at some point during the evening, Joel asked if he could say something. You could have heard a pin drop! What was he going to say? How would my children react? I was caught completely off guard. "I just want you all to know that you don't have to worry about your mother. I care about her and I have no intention of hurting her." I know only a few second went by, but it seemed like forever. The room was silent. Then Christopher walked across the room and shook Joel's hand. It felt like a seal of approval; I smiled and took a breath. It's quite an experience when the tables are turned and the *children* are vetting a parent's partner choice. I never expected the myriad of feelings that came over me those few days.

We left for home New Year's Eve afternoon. One of the nicest pictures I have of the two of us was taken that night by our waiter at a restaurant in Orlando. We spent New Year's Day at Universal in Orlando before heading back to Lake Placid.

Here's where things become a little fuzzy... maybe because I feel like Joel and I have been together forever and everything runs together.

Only six weeks later, we became engaged: February 14, 2011, Valentine's Day. What happened over those six weeks? We saw a lot of each other. We talked on the phone a lot. I admit that I did spend a couple of weekends with him, but I knew it wasn't the right thing to do. Did I think getting married soon would solve that problem? Sure, I did, but that's not a reason to get married. We have both had experienced painful divorces and we wanted to make sure we knew what we were doing. But...truth is...we almost knew the day we met.

I remember looking at the calendar in my office the day after we got engaged. Joel was happy with a little *longer* engagement, but I knew I couldn't very well move in with him and plan a long engagement. That wouldn't work. I scanned the months of March...April...May. That was long enough. "How about May 14th?" I said. I think Joel was a little surprised, but he agreed. And then the plans began.

The months of Sundays before the wedding were actually funny. People would sit in the parish hall and watch when I came in to church...and when Joel came into church. Was he in *his* car? Did they come *together?* Then there were the little old ladies that accosted him regularly, telling him that 'you'd better not hurt her!' I think most guys would have left. But not this one!

My first choice to preside over our marriage was Bishop Howe. But it wasn't to be. And I think I knew it before I even asked. I knew he had uncompromising views about divorce, and even though he knows God forgives, his feelings are strong regarding the sacrament of marriage. It made me sad, but I understood. I remember the day he called me. I walked into the garage at Joel's house. He asked how we were, and then he said, "You know I can't marry you..." He did indeed sound sad when he said it, but it was a choice he had to make.

My thought fell to Fr. Edward Weiss, and it was indeed my best choice. Edward and I used to ride together to diocesan meetings. I would drive forty minutes to Okeechobee and ride the other hour with him to Orlando. We shared much on those rides. He became a spiritual director of sorts and helped me through lots of issues over many years. He was the perfect choice for pre-marital conversations as well as nuptials.

I think this was going really fast for Joel. Poor guy, but he trusted his gut and he trusted God. When we saw Edward that first time, his first words to Joel were, "Are you ready for this partnership?" and he wasn't talking about marriage. Marrying a priest comes with a lot of responsibility as well as its own call. That question laid heavy on Joel for a long time before he really talked about it, but he knew he was ready from the first.

One thing that stands out for me during this preparation time was a DVD that Edward had given us. It was a Charles Spurgeon teaching on marriage and it hit me like a gut punch! I was watching it one evening and the tears began to fall from my eyes. His explanation of sex before marriage was so powerful, so incredibly holy, that I realized we had to make a change. I so wanted God's blessing on our marriage. I was convinced that God had put us together for his purpose and we couldn't do anything to jeopardize that gift. So celibacy was the order of the day until we married. Difficult, but possible, and we knew God was with us.

My parish took on the responsibility of our wedding, and it couldn't have been any more beautiful. Everything was planned for us...the reception, the cakes (the traditional wedding cake along with the groom's cake—a chain saw!) Pictures were taken. The hall was prepared. The parish was invited. The only thing Joel and I did was purchase multiple heavy hors-d'oeuvres the week before the wedding. And the story of that trip to Costco's will go down through the ages...

Since the parish was invited as well as the guests who received invitations, we really had no idea how many people would attend. So we really had no option for the reception except to serve heavy hors d'oeuvres. So Joel and I went to Costco's the Saturday morning before the wedding. Before we left the house I grabbed a couple of Hershey's kisses from the bowl on the table. We stopped for breakfast on the way. I did eat at least one on the way, but apparently a couple of them fell out of my pocket. When we got back in the truck after breakfast, there was a mess of melted chocolate on my seat! Horrified, I cleaned it up and I said to Joel, "Please tell me that I don't have chocolate on my pants!" He said very emphatically: "You don't have chocolate on your pants!" Relieved, I finished cleaning up the seat, got in, we went to

Costco's, and left with two overflowing, grocery carts. We put everything in the truck and headed for home.

When we got home, I changed my clothes and just about had a stroke! The back of my pants were all full of melted chocolate! I screamed: "I asked you if..." Joel cut me off in mid sentence and said, "No, you didn't *ask*...you said '*tell* me I don't have chocolate on my pants', and that's exactly what I did." That was the week before the wedding. The wedding still went off as planned!

It was indeed a beautiful day—May 14, 2011. Joel's three daughters were there; all our church family was there and many friends came as well. It wasn't a good time of year for my children...end of the school year and other issues making travel impossible. But it was really fine. I thought I'd feel sad because they weren't there, but truth be told, it was *our* day and that made it right. There was no wedding party. All that was needed was two persons to sign the marriage license. The church was full, the music was beautiful and the ceremony was perfect. We had both waited a long time for this kind of happiness... and it had finally arrived. *With God, all things are possible!*

CHAPTER 11

705 Jefferson Avenue,
Lehigh Acres, Florida

> A large three-bedroom, two-bath home with a dining room, two living rooms, a big man-cave, complete with a pool table and bar. A beautiful swimming pool and a garage, complete with half-built trucks! Not much landscaping...that came later...

The day I came to Joel's home that Thanksgiving, I remember thinking how lovely it was. I was impressed. I did learn, however, that he'd had some help from his sister. Still I was looking forward to adding my personal touch. He had lived there for quite a few years, and while the inside was quite attractive, the outside was somewhat plain, devoid of plants and flowers. We talked about just that several times and little by little, I added my touch. One night sitting at the dinner table, talking about some of the things I had added, Joel's comment brought tears to my eyes: "I worked very hard to give you a blank canvas," he said, "and now it's bursting with color, warmth and happiness. I knew some day I'd have someone to share it with, and I'm very, very happy with our life together. It couldn't be more comfortable. It's *our* home."

As I think about my life over the past ten years, I marvel at the presence of God through it all. We worked through issues that come along with blended families. We worked together at St. Francis, continuing what had been done in the past and improving things for the future. And I learned how special it is to have someone by your side through everything that life throws at you. He supports my vocation and he has *his own* sense of service to the Lord. He treats me as an equal and he loves me unconditionally. God heard my prayers and he answered in an unexpected way, including living in a house with a "man cave!"

After Joel and I were married, I now had a sixty-five-mile commute to and from my parish. Luckily it was an easy ride, little traffic to deal with. During those first couple of years, I was amazed at the comments from my parishioners about how I had changed...how I seemed to be so happy...how happy they were for me. They more than accepted Joel into our parish family and he gladly accepted them...even the ones who had originally threatened him!

Many of my parishioners had been there almost from the beginning of my ministry among them, and they saw things that I never realized. It's funny that when you think you're hiding things from other people, it often turns out that everybody knew what you thought was hidden. It reminded me of forty years ago, how I tried to protect my young children from all the hurts that come with a divorce...and it didn't work. They noticed more than I realized and it affected them in later years. I hope their hurts have healed today. Perhaps my earlier experiences in this book will be helpful.

St. Francis of Assisi Church
Lake Placid, Florida

One of my big take-aways at this point in my life is the importance of spousal support...for *all* couples. Making any marriage work, being equal partners, is a job in itself, let alone being a clergy spouse, My Joel, however, handles it with ease. It was just another of the many puzzle pieces that God put together for both of us. God had prepared me for an unconditional relationship with a wonderful man, and God had prepared Joel for a new and demanding position in life that he accepted with no reservation. Our time together at St. Francis was very special. We gave witness to a marriage, founded and based on the truths of our faith, and we shared our blessing with all those we knew. Wherever we are led in the future, we know the plan is already laid out and it will be under God's direction.

I began this writing sometime before my approaching retirement: December 31, 2019. Retirement? How can that be? Twenty-one years have passed and the mandatory age of retirement—72—is close at hand. So the year 2019 would be a year of planning, making sure whatever legacy I leave behind is the best I can accomplish. Surprisingly, 2019 went quite smoothly even though it was a little scary. It wasn't always easy to know that St. Francis would be part of my past, but I knew that God would have other plans for me. Little did I know…

The parish did an amazing job on that special day—December 29, 2019. Three of my children and their families were with me and it will always be a day to remember, and if I even *begin* to forget, I'll refer to the newspaper article that was in the paper; it was a full two-page story, complete with pictures! There is no chance of forgetting one of the most rewarding days of my life, getting to see those persons who helped make me the person I was meant to be.

Final Service at St. Francis – December 29, 2019

Probably the greatest thing I've learned in my journey thus far is the importance of the presence of God in every part of my life. He was always there, whether I acknowledged Him or not. There was joy when we were connected; there was turmoil when we were distant. It's simple, really, and it's that complicated. The key is God.

159

My second important teacher was Joel. I've learned so much from him. First and foremost, I finally learned the meaning of joy... *not* the word that we connect with being happy, but the joy that we identify with the Spirit of God. It's called a "fruit" of the Spirit. No matter what the day had brought, his dinner prayers were *always* filled with thanksgiving and joy. It's that special joy that Paul had, even when he was in chains. He wrote about it to those he loved. He understood the presence of God in all facets of life...so does Joel.

I've learned what it means to be part of a team, to have everything in common, to seek the good in each other and forgive easily. That can only be done when each person knows who they are, and *whose* they are.

When I began this book, I had no idea how difficult it was going to be. There were times when I had to stop writing because *remembering* brought back hurts I had chosen to forget. We don't willingly recall those things in our lives that hurt us. But while there were parts of this book that were extremely painful to recall, I was driven to write, and it became a labor of love.

In case you're wondering why I would share such personal details with you, the answer is simple: Encouragement. The only way to encourage someone else is to be vulnerable. There is strength in vulnerability. Think about it. The world wants you to believe that being vulnerable is a weakness. Nothing could be further from the truth. It takes courage and strength to be vulnerable, and I hope this book gives you the courage you need on your journey.

Whether you know it or not, we're on this journey together, you and I. If you're reading this, you are my family, a close friend, or maybe even a new friend, and God has placed us side by side to support each other, to encourage each other, and to love each other blindly. We are meant to carry each other's burdens, to love each other no matter what, to be there when times are joyful and to hold each other up when life is hell. If we can get beyond those things that divide us, love, joy, and harmony will abound.

It's okay to show weakness, because I'll be right there to give you support without judgment. It's okay to be honest with those you

160

love, because if they *truly* love you, you'll be encouraged, not belittled.

Time after time, over all these years, everything that happened to me—good and bad—was part of God's plan...the plan to form me into the person I am today. And if you take nothing else away from this book, know that God has a plan for you too. Your job is to let God *be* God. Depend on Him from the moment you wake up in the morning until you close your eyes at night. He loves you more than you can imagine. You are forgiven because you were made in His Image, and he can do nothing less!

May your journey through life be blessed. May you draw strength from your times of trial. And may you always know that God is by your side.

"For surely I know the plans
I have for you, says the Lord,
plans for your welfare
and not for harm,
to give you a future with hope.
Then when you call upon me
and come and pray to me,
I will hear you. When you search for me,
you will find me;
if you seek me with all your heart,
I will let you find me,"
says the Lord...
Jeremiah 29:11-14a

EPILOGUE

At the end of this book's introduction, I wrote: *Truth be told, God was at the helm from the beginning, whether I knew it or not, and even with my missteps, His plan was accomplished...*

Even as I completed this book, *God's work* wasn't finished. As Joel and I searched for a church in which to worship, God placed us in the midst of a small community of faith— Good Shepherd Episcopal Church—that was on the verge of closing. But there was more work to be done.

I became Priest-in-charge of the small congregation and today we're doubled in size, potentially growing right through the coronavirus pandemic! How long will I be there? God will surely let me know...He hasn't led me astray yet.

ABOUT THE AUTHOR

Elizabeth L. Nelson is an Episcopal priest, a wife, a mother, a grandmother, and a great-grandmother. Accomplishments were not grand, but they were fulfilling. After a short but successful career in the business world, she was called, in her late thirties, to become a priest. She served as rector of a church in Central Florida for twenty-one years and following retirement, is presently priest-in-charge of a small church in Southwest Florida.

She enjoys doing needlepoint, writing, gardening, reading and spending time with family and friends in Florida and Rhode Island.